THE LOGIC OF ABELARD

SYNTHESE HISTORICAL LIBRARY

TEXTS AND STUDIES IN THE HISTORY OF

LOGIC AND PHILOSOPHY

HUMANITIES PRESS/NEW YORK

MARIA TERESA
BEONIO-BROCCHIERI FUMAGALLI

THE LOGIC OF ABELARD

D. REIDEL PUBLISHING COMPANY/DORDRECHT-HOLLAND

LA LOGICA DI ABELARDO
Published by La Nuova Italia Editrice, Firenze, 1969 (2nd Edition)
Translated from the Italian by
Simon Pleasance, for Intercontinental Translators (City) Co.

SOLE DISTRIBUTORS FOR U.S.A. AND CANADA
HUMANITIES PRESS/NEW YORK

Printed in The Netherlands by D. Reidel, Dordrecht

PREMISE

The purely 'philosophical' importance of logical Abelardian research has been emphasized by Mario Dal Pra in his introduction to the edition of the *Glosse Letterali*. In this volume it seems important in my eyes to illustrate not only the interest of Abelardian dialectic techniques (which are at times penetrated by positions which are still realistic), but also, and above all, the importance of his total attitude towards the 'scientia scientiarum', stated in advance by a freer and braver mentality that is later to use this instrument for its rigorous definition of philosophical research.

When studying Abelardian dialectic I have preferred to follow the line of development of his inquiry, from meaning to syllogistic calculation. This line does not, however, coincide perfectly with the expositive progress of the various commentaries, from the *Isagoge* to the Boetian texts; the trail has thus been marked out for me by some of the Palatine Master's statements rather than by the order of the comments.

The perspective of this research is, generally speaking, given from the viewpoint of contemporary formal logic, a viewpoint that is nevertheless implicit, even, I think, if it is at work in inquiry. In fact, in an attempt to have a clearer picture of the historical importance of the author and his meaning in a dialogue which is mediaeval, I have tried, as far as possible, to keep the language constantly in the tone of those times, and I have tried to avoid certain equations – unprecise and sterile in my opinion – between Abelardian logical formulae and contemporary logical formulae. I hope that what will be of interest from a modern viewpoint is Abelard's total attitude.

FOREWORD TO THE SECOND EDITION

The delicacy – and at times the ambivalence – of the Abelardian position in the logical debate of his time has recently been brought to light by De Rijk in his work *Logica Modernorum*: the weight of the metaphysical perspective and the lack of a clear cut with the psychological and gnoseological implications of the theory of the *significatio* do not, however, exclude the presence of a *contextual approach* in the Palatine Master's attitude.

I think, therefore, that an analytical reading of Abelard's philosophical texts is an important, indeed obligatory, step in the study of the birth and development both of the *suppositio* theory and of terminist logic on the whole.

Milan, March 1969

TABLE OF CONTENTS

INTRODUCTION

The importance of Pierre Abelard's position in the history of logic has been stressed by the editions of the *Glosse Letterali* edited by M. Dal Pra[1], of the *Dialectica* edited by De Rijk[2], and, more recently by the publication of two texts which Minio Paluello attributes to the Palatine Master.[3]

The interest of students in the writings of Abelard is further stimulated by considering the time in which he lived, a strategic point in the history of mediaeval logic; also by the echo of the fame in which his contemporaries had cloaked him, and by his own vivacious and rampant personality.

The historical *humus* which nourished and fired the polemic that makes the Palatine Master's pages so personal and noteworthy is not yet completely known to us, and Geyer has already pointed out the difficulty of satisfactorily understanding the logical position of Abelard before being familiar with the contemporary glossary material.[4] This material, judging by the information supplied to us by John of Salisbury and by the actual words of our subject, who tells us of numerous discussions and frequently refers to the 'sententiae' of 'quidam' which give a different interpretation of the Aristotelian or Boetian passages, turned out to be of considerable weight.

We know that Abelard was a pupil of Roscellin and Guillaume de Champeaux, and thus in a position to glean the opposite and salient motifs of the polemic on universals. This possibly contributed to the opinion that the Abelardian position in the classical discussion 'de generibus' of the 12th century had a conciliatory effect between the extreme positions of the two masters: Cousin's verdict on Abelardian 'conceptualism'[5] provided the justificative basis of what was to become one of the common places of textbooks of the history of philosophy.

These and other considerations, which were found to be somewhat arbitrary and hasty (like Prantl's statement that Abelard the dialectic had a fundamentally rhetorical spirit[6]) originated above all from the inadequacy of the accessible texts before Geyer's editions, which gave the first decisive stimulus to the study of the Palatine Master's philosophical writings.

Up to 1919 (the year of Geyer's first edition) the known Abelardian writings were limited to those edited by Cousin[7]: this French scholar attached the most importance to the comments on Porphyrius, the *Categorie* and the *Topici* of Boetius and the passages of the *Dialectica*. On the whole the material was fragmentary, uncritically sifted and confused with fragments of non-Abelardian comments, which Cousin nonetheless considered were his. De Remusat's incomplete paraphrase in French of a comment on the *Isagoge* was then added to these texts.

In 1919 Geyer began publishing *Ingredientibus*[8]: under this name he has edited a comment on the *Isagoge*, a second on the *Categorie*, and a third on *De Interpretatione*. A prologue (from the beginning of which Geyer took the name *Ingredientibus*) presents these comments as a unit which has a certain compactness; this is confirmed by other observations which are intrinsic to the work, such as the internal cross-references from comment to comment, the persistence of a similar attitude and of an identical – terminologically as well – solution when confronted by the problem of universals in all the comments[9], the 'dictum' theory present in the three comments.[10] From internal cross-references that Abelard makes to an essay *De Hypotheticis*[11], Geyer concludes that the work must have included other comments as well as these. From hints dropped by Abelard in *De Interpretatione*, it seems highly likely to me that a comment on *De Categoricis* also belonged to *Ingredientibus*.[12] Dal Pra has shown that the comment on *De differentiis topicis*, edited by him, is clearly distinct from the literal comments, and concluded that this is a comment that comes within the framework of *Ingredientibus*.[13] We thus have four of the seven comments on the usual 'septem codices'[14] that Abelard considered fundamental.

Also part of the *Philosophische Schriften* edited by Geyer is a comment on the *Isagoge* of which Remusat had edited an incomplete paraphrase in French. In the prologue Geyer singled it out as part of an organic work, called *Nostrorum*[15] by him from the words at the beginning: here too Abelard proposed an entire treatment of the logical *corpus* usually used by him. Today we still have only the comment on the Porphyrian *quinque voces*.

In 1954 Geyer's edition was joined by the edition of the literal comments edited by M. Dal Pra. In this edition the comments are arranged in the order which Abelard himself indicates at the end of the logical treatise and to which he also holds in *Dialectica*. The comments on the *Categorie* and on *De Interpretatione* thus come after the comment on the *Isagoge*. The presence of a comment on the Boetian *De Divisionibus* indicates that Abelard used the 'seven codes' from the outset and leads one reasonably to suppose that he had worked on other comments of the same type as *De Syllogismis categoricis*, *De Syllogismis Hypotheticis*, and *De Differentiis topicis* which we do not have now. This seems to me to be confirmed by certain references of *Dialectica*, which are remade in the comments on *De Differentiis topicis* and *De hypotheticis* in the *Introductiones parvulorum*[16], identified by Geyer with the literal notes. We have already seen how the comment on *De Differentiis topicis* edited by Dal Pra in the *Scritti Filosofici* must be assimilated, on the contrary, to the *corpus* of notes in *Ingredientibus*.

In 1956 De Rijk published an edition of *Dialectica* which enhances the picture of the Palatine Master's logical work. *Dialectica* is not a comment but an organic treatise based nonetheless on the 'septem codices'. The most serious gap, by extension and importance, is that which deprives us of the treatise on the Porphyrian *quinque voces* which was certainly included in the work, because Abelard hints at it. Two passages in this work show us Abelard's concept of it[17]: the Palatine Master here presented himself as an *auctor* in line with Aristotle, Porphyrius and Boetius, whose works he would perfect, as he proudly declares.

In *Abaelardiana inedita* edited by Minio Paluello[18], two texts are edited, the first contained in a manuscript now in Berlin, and the second belonging to a manuscript in the monastery of Fleury, both from the 12th century. The existence of these two manuscripts was not unknown to us.[19] The text of the Berlin manuscript, a commentary on *De Interpretatione*, is three-quarters identical to the Ambrosian manuscript edited by Geyer as a section of *Ingredientibus* and the part that differs is without any doubt more coherent with the preceding part than the Ambrosian manuscript which contained a noteworthy break. The contribution of this new edition consists in a rigour and a greater accuracy in the reading of the Abelardian text: it does not, however, appear that in this last part of the commentary there are motives that complete or at least modify the weight and the general meaning of the commentary itself.

The text of the Fleury manuscript is more interesting, even if, with regard to the attribution, it is more uncertain. This concerns the analysis of a paralogism and of five sophisms that emerge from a nominalistic interpretation of the concept of *totum*.

The problem of establishing the chronological relation between various Abelardian works is quite complex. Broadly speaking, the Abelardian logical works seem to have come about through the literal comments, with *Ingredientibus*, *Nostrorum*, and *Dialectica* as the culmination of the author's maturity. But we have known for some time that the relation between the last three works is not at all clear.

The order indicated before is mainly a logical order which also has some chronological value: the literal notes, as we shall see, present, in the simple form of the comment adhering to the text of authority, some interesting and coherent positions; they are texts belonging to the period of the first dialectic instruction during which the exercise of explanation was to prevail over personal development of a theme and constitute the necessary premise for wider and more original work. Dal Pra suggests that the notes of this type were compiled in the period from 1102–05 to 1112–14.[20]

Having patronised the basic matter, the seven codes, Abelard proceeded to a form of fuller and more liberated comment.

Ingredientibus comes after the *Introductiones parvulorum*, that is sure: the acritical position taken of the latter has become explicit in the articulate discussion of the former. With regard to the problem of dating *Ingredientibus*, two opinions have been formed to date: Geyer's, which is based on the comparison with other, and also theological, texts, opts for a dating before 1120[21]; and D'Olwer's, based on references made by Abelard at Nantes, which suggests c. 1110 for *Ingredientibus*, because Abelard was very probably living in Brittany at that time.[22] The two viewpoints are not opposed; but the date of the composition of *Ingredientibus* is too indeterminate, and in addition D'Olwer's observation which sees the work composed c. 1110 perhaps overlooks the differences, not to say arrangement, in style between the literal notes and the comment on *Ingredientibus*.[23] But an even greater problem arises when one examines the comment *De Differentiis topicis*, which, as Dal Pra has surely shown, belongs to the same work and which, according to Geyer, would have been composed after 1121.[24] This would lead to a break of composition – an inadmissible break – in a work that is conspicuous for its unity of character, style and 'density' of comment and coherence of positions; even the chronological relation with *Nostrorum* is not at all definite.

But, as D'Olwer[25] has observed, the criterion followed by Geyer with regard to *De Differentiis topicis* should not represent a fixed rule; it is also true, furthermore, that D'Olwer's observation about Nantes, mentioned in *Ingredientibus*, does not offer a sound enough basis for any chronological indication, also because it is not certain whether Abelard went to Brittany in 1110.

As far as I can see, one must take into account: (a) the difference between the characters which inspire the literal notes and *Ingredientibus*; (b) two passages from *Dialectica* (to which we shall refer presently), the first draft of which D'Olwer fixes before 1118, which, when compared with two parallel passages in *Ingredientibus*, show an evidently immature formulation[26]; (c) a passage in *Ingredientibus*, which shows an affinity with the exposition of the 'totus' theory contained in *Dialectica*, and is possibly an implicit reply to the sarcastic remarks in one of Roscellin's letters which was definitely written after 1118.[27] All these things would tend to confirm the hypothesis that the *Ingredientibus* was written in c. 1120.

Opinions differ less on the chronology of *Nostrorum*: again basing his argument on the comparison with theological texts, Geyer puts its composition some time after 1120[28]; D'Olwer agrees and puts these notes on a parallel with the second edition of *Dialectica* (1121–23).[29] This date can be further confirmed if we consider that the difficult situation in which Abelard found himself after the sentence of Soissons and his desire to distinguish his own terminology from Roscellin's might offer a valid reason for forcing him to the *vox-sermo* distinction in *Nostrorum*. The proximity of the two dates of composition of *Ingredientibus* and *Nostrorum* does not in my eyes pose any problems: as we shall see, the two works offer fairly identical solutions to the *quaestio de universalibus*, and the difference in terminology is explicable if we consider that the *vox-sermo* distinction was already prepared in the first text.[30] Moreover this terminological isolation of *Nostrorum* would suggest that Abelard was driven to use new terms as a result of a contingent reason that did not require a revision of positions as much as an exact definition of formulation.

The dating of *Dialectica* is more complicated. Contrary to Cousin and Geyer, who are of the opinion that the text of *Dialectica* was composed with chronological unity[31], D'Olwer and Cottiaux claim they can single out three successive drafts in it. But D'Olwer does not agree with Cottiaux over the dates of the three drafts or over the division of the matter[32], and reaches the conclusion that a first draft was made before the tragic incident that separated Abelard from Heloïse, namely before 1118; and further that Abelard then took up the work again between 1121 and 1123 and that the third revision of *Dialectica* was finally completed in 1135–37. The evidence used by D'Olwer has already been to some extent criticised by De Rijk[33], and one might perhaps go further with the indication that D'Olwer draws from the presence of the name Guillaume in the first treatise, but this would not conclusively establish a precise date; however, a full reading of the 1956 edition of *Dialectica* (an edition which D'Olwer did not know) can only confirm the impression of a so-to-speak stratified composition, suggested by the language used, which is not as typicised as in either *Ingredientibus* or *Nostrorum*.[34]

Some parallel passages and others in *Ingredientibus* appear to me, however, to offer a relevant proof of the irregularity of the composition. Consider the *dictum* theory which is expounded in *Ingredientibus* in a definitely more explicit, mature and critical manner than in *Dialectica*[35]; and likewise the *quaestio de maximis propositionibus*, the discussion of which in *Dialectica* gives rise to more than one perplexity and is, in any event, less clear, less linear and less mature than in the comment.[36] There are, moreover, two passages in *Ingredientibus* (on the contingent future and the *dictiones indefinitae*)[37] with a more backward formulation when compared with the two analogous sections of *Dialectica* which show a marked progress in the line of discussion.[38] The complex of the passages quoted confirms the opinion of a stratified composition in *Dialectica*, and not only this, it induces, in my opinion, a revision of the chronological relation which has not to date been discussed. That is to say, the two passages on the *dictum* and the *maximae propositiones* appear to indicate that the draft of *Dialectica* as regards these arguments came before the composition of *Ingredientibus*; this should not appear strange if we accept D'Olwer's thesis, which is particularly reliable on this point, that the first draft of *Dialectica* goes back to before 1118, and if we remember that complex of reasons which makes us prefer the years around 1120 rather than D'Olwer's 1110 for the chronology of *Ingredientibus*.

Abelard himself indicates which are the logical texts that he considers fundamental[39] and on which all his works, comments and free treatments unfold along precise lines.

We can point out, above all, the texts which are indisputably acquainted with Abelard's works, first and foremost the Porphyrian *Isagoge*. The Boetian notes are a guide to his comment to Porphyrius.[40] We have two comments by Boetius on the *De quinque vocibus* treatise[41], and from two Abelardian passages we can be reasonably sure that the Palatine Master worked on both comments. In the first Boetian comment, guided by Vittorino's translation, we find the term *sermo* used to indicate the noun, not the discourse[42]: this might have been the cue[43] which prompted Abelard to his wide use of this term[44] in *Nostrorum* in an accepted meaning which was not the common one.[45]

In the second comment the passage of interest is the one concerning the theory of abstraction seen as that intellectual operation that can abstract from any aspect of the real.[46] It is quite probable that this Boetian hint is the suggestion that Abelard takes into consideration in his exposition of the doctrine of abstraction[47], which, in as far as it is not in contrast with the Aristotelian doctrine, nonetheless shows aspects which do not derive directly from Aristotle.[48]

Another text that Abelard honours among those which "usus adhuc latinorum cognovit" is Aristotle's *Categorie*. As in the previous text, we can observe that all three treatments in our hands on the categories[49] are guided by Aristotle's texts through the comment by Boetius.[50]

Aristotle's other text of which "eloquentia latina armatur" is the Periermeneias.[51]

Four Boetian texts figure among the seven basic codes: *Liber Divisionum* and *Topicorum*, *De Syllogismis categoricis*, and *De Syllogismis hypotheticis*.[52] In the first and the second we have a comment and a more autonomous treatment.[53] The other two texts are the basis of two sections in *Dialectica*: the third book of the second treatise[54] and the first and second books of the fourth treatise, respectively.[55]

These are the seven canonical texts which, in a statement by Abelard himself, constitute the logical *corpus* that the Latins used as a rule.

It is harder to determine if and to what extent Abelard was acquainted with other Aristotelian works. This is given added interest because it is certain that at the time in which Abelard worked the *Topici* and the *Elenchi Sofistici* were already in circulation and were used by Adam Parvipontanus in his *Ars Disserendi*[56], and that Abelard himself shows an acquaintance with the arguments

dealt with by Aristotle in other works of the *Organon*. One can
divide the passages that contain references to the remaining Aristotelian texts into three groups: in the first group we can place those
that suggest that the Palatine Master was familiar with the argument
in Aristotle's books not used by him; in the second those that
show that he had direct knowledge of some texts; and lastly we
shall point out a statement that shows that Abelard was erroneously
informed about some parts of these books.

(a) In both *Ingredientibus*[57] and *Nostrorum*[58] Abelard shows a
certain knowledge of the content of Aristotle's *Topica* and *Analytica*:
these hints are, however, too generic to be the basis for the hypothesis that he had a direct and even complete knowledge of them.
This in fact hinges not on quotations but on indications of arguments treated in the two works without precise reference to the
order in which these subjects are unfolded in the Aristotelian text.

(b) Indication of a direct knowledge is, however, given in a
passage in the comment on *De Interpretatione* of *Ingredientibus*,
in which Abelard says he recalls having read one of Aristotle's
'small works' called *Elenchi Sofistici*.[59] But this is not enough:
precisely with regard to this Abelard (justly) corrects a statement by
Boetius about a direct reference to the *Elenchi Sofistici*, and in the
middle comment he refers back to Aristotle's words in this text.[60]
Two passages of *Dialectica*, pointed out by Geyer and one by
De Rijk[61], which probably derive directly from the *Primi Analitici*,
should be added to this group.

(c) The passages of the third group are interesting because they
seem to jeopardise the hypotheses that we shall try to draw from
the evidence listed in (b). These are hints contained in the comment
on *De Interpretatione* of *Ingredientibus*, on the material of a part
of the *Primi* and *Secondi Analitici*.[62] The cross-reference, as observed by Geyer[63], is partly wrong, and Abelard shows not only
that he is acquainted with the *Analitici Secondi* but also that he is
partially informed on the *Primi*.

The passages we have placed in group (a) cannot be used as
proof in favour of a direct acquaintance, because, due to their
generic aspect, they might derive from quotations that Boetius

makes in the texts with which we know Abelard was acquainted.[64] The evidence of group (b) seems on the other hand to indicate with some certainty that Abelard had seen the *Elenchi Sofistici* and part of the *Primi Analitici* (not in their totality, as is shown by the error made by Abelard in the quotations of group (c)), but above all that the circulation of the *Elenchi Sofistici* was limited and acquaintance with them was not usual. This incidentally agrees with the tone of Abelard's statement concerning the logical texts normally used by students and scholars as the thread of their inquiries: an affirmation that does not exclude an as it were 'occasional' acquaintance with other texts and a marginal exploitation of them.[65] Abelard is on the threshold of an age that becomes more and more animated by new sources and suggestions for research: his instruments are still the traditional ones, but he is already participating, if only in part, in the discoveries of texts which start to circulate again, extending the field of inquiry and rendering discussion more articulate and comprehensive.

REFERENCES

[1] *Scritti filosofici*, Milan 1954. These will be abbreviated to *G.L.*
[2] *Dialectica*, Assen 1956. Second, reviced edition, Assen 1969. This will be abbreviated to *D.*
[3] *Abaelardiana inedita*, Rome 1958.
[4] Geyer, *Untersuchungen*, *Beiträge*, XIII, 1933.
[5] Cousin, *Ouvrages inédits d'Abelard*, Paris 1836, p. CLVI.
[6] Prantl, *Storia della logica in Occidente, Età medievale*, Florence 1937, pp. 304–8.
[7] Cousin, *op. cit.*, and *Petri Abaelardi opera hactenus seorsim edita...*, Paris 1859.
[8] *Philosophische Schriften*, Münster 1919, 1921, 1927. Abbreviated to *G.G.*
[9] See *G.G.*, pp. 16, 127, 403, and *G.L.*, p. 235; *G.G.*, pp. 38, 246, 334–5, and *G.L.*, p. 221.
[10] See p. 79, note 39.
[11] *G.G.*, pp. 291 (25) and 389 (7).
[12] *G.G.*, p. 394 (10–26).
[13] Dal Pra, 'Introduzione', in *G.L.*, pp. xxix–xxxii.
[14] *D.*, p. 146 (10–7).
[15] *G.G.*, p. 505 (3–5).
[16] *D.*, pp. 269 (1–3), 329 (4), 482 (4–6).
[17] *D.*, pp. 146 (10–20), 496 (18–26).

[18] *Abaelardiana inedita*, Rome 1958.

[19] *Id.*, pp. xiiff., xli.

[20] Dal Pra, *op.cit.*, p. XIII.

[21] Geyer, *op.cit.*, pp. 598–602.

[22] D'Olwer, 'Sur la date de la Dialectique d'Abelard', *Revue du Moyen Age*, 1945, Nr. 1, p. 389.

[23] One can see, for example, the acritical and yet nominalistic position of Abelard in the literal notes (see pp. 39-40): this would seem to indicate an influence of the Roscellinian solution on the young master of dialectic who would only have felt himself ready for taking up an explicit and personal stand in *Ingredientibus*, and therefore certainly some years later.

[24] Geyer, *op.cit.*, p. 606.

[25] D'Olwer, *op.cit.*, p. 376.

[26] See pp. 65-8 with regard to the passages which refer to the 'dictum' theory, and pp. 77-9 for the 'quaestio de maximis propositionibus' discussed both in *Ingredientibus* and *Dialectica*.

[27] *G.G.*, pp. 104 (26)–105 (38), and *D.*, p. 552 (15ff.). Prantl, *op.cit.*, p. 141, note 314.

[28] Geyer, *op.cit.*, pp. 602–3.

[29] D'Olwer, *op.cit.*, p. 390.

[30] See pp. 47, 55–56, and 69, note 94.

[31] D'Olwer, *op.cit.*, p. 375.

[32] *Id.*, p. 376.

[33] De Rijk, 'Introduction', in *D.*, pp. xxii, note 9, and xvii, note 3.

[34] For example to indicate the universal in *Dialectica* Abelard uses "nomen, dictio, vocabulum et vox". But consider the remark on p. 59.

[35] See pp. 72 and 74–75.

[36] See pp. 86–87.

[37] *G.G.*, pp. 419ff., 337ff.

[38] *D.*, pp. 210–22, 118–20.

[39] *D.*, p. 146 (10–7).

[40] De Rijk, *op.cit.*, p. xiii.

[41] Gilson, *La philosophie au moyen âge*, Paris 1934, p. 139; cf. Boetius, *P.L.*, p. LXIV.

[42] Boetius, *P.L.*, pp. LXIV, 19.

[43] 'Sermo' used as 'nomen' is nevertheless present elsewhere in Boetius (*P.L.*, pp. LXI, 169). Notwithstanding, before Reiners (*Der Nominalismus in der Frühscholastik*, Münster 1910) noted and specified the accepted meaning of this term, neither Prantl nor Remusat had thought it could be translated other than by 'discourse' or 'judgement'.

[44] *G.G.*, pp. 522ff.

[45] Abelard uses this term in the commonly accepted meaning in *G.L.*, p. 299 (10).

[46] Boetius, *P.L.*, pp. LXIV, 84.

[47] *G.G.*, pp. 25ff.

[48] Gilson, *op.cit.*, p. 287.

[49] *G.L.*, pp. 43–67; *G.G.*, pp. 111–305; *D.*, pp. 51–110.

[50] The question of the editions of the Boetian commentary has been approached and discussed by Minio Paluello and De Rijk (De Rijk, *op.cit.*, pp. xiii–xvi,

and Minio Paluello, 'Note sull' Aristotele latino medievale', *Riv. di Fil. Neo-Scol.*, 1958 Nr. 10, pp. 110–11 and Nr. 11, pp. 217–48).

[51] *D.*, p. 146 (10–2).

[52] *D.*, p. 146 (10–2).

[53] *G.L.*, pp. 155–203; *D.*, pp. 535–98; *G.L.*, pp. 205–330; *D.*, pp. 263–413.

[54] *D.*, pp. 232–51.

[55] *D.*, pp. 479–533.

[56] Minio Paluello, 'Adam of Balsham "Parvipontanus"', *Mediaeval and Renaissance Studies*, 1954, p. 3, pp. 136ff. See also De Rijk, *op.cit.*, p. xix.

[57] *G.G.*, p. 2 (12–5); *G.G.*, p. 111 (11–2); *G.L.*, p. 213 (1–5); less noteworthy are the references in *G.G.*, p. 319 (18–9) and in *G.G.*, p. 455 (35ff.). Note also in *Abael. inedita* the reference to the *Analitici* on p. 10 (22) and the references to the *Elenchi Sofistici* on pp. 13 (17) and 30 (29) belonging to the comment on *De Interpretatione*.

[58] *G.G.*, p. 509 (1–8).

[59] *G.G.*, p. 400 (33ff.).

[60] *G.G.*, pp. 400 (2ff.) and 489 (2ff.).

[61] De Rijk, *op.cit.*, p. xvii. As for the identifications of the 'translationes' on which Abelard most likely worked, see De Rijk again, who re-uses the considerations of Geyer and Minio Paluello on this point (*op.cit.*, p. xviii).

[62] *G.G.*, p. 394 (10–25).

[63] *G.G.*, p. 394 note 1.

[64] De Rijk, *op.cit.*, p. xvii.

[65] The term 'usus' in the expression "usus adhuc Latinorum cognovit" (*D.*, p. 146 (10–2)) is interpreted, as Geyer and De Rijk observed, as 'traditional basis of doctrine' rather than as 'knowledge'. In this sense this would mean not only that the traditional 'corpus' does not exhaust the whole of the known texts, but also suggests a wider availability of texts which are not usually used to advantage. The expression 'quidam libellus' referred to the *Elenchi Sofistici* (see note 59) is evidence of this limited knowledge and use.

CHAPTER I

WHAT ABELARD MEANS BY LOGIC

Abelard's defence of logic in *Dialectica* pivots on one basic point: its 'scientia' and consequently its incompatibility with the attribute of 'mala', an attribute that can only be due to the 'exercitium' of science.[1]

It is, for this reason, interesting to establish first of all the position that logical 'scientia' occupies in the general framework of knowledge and what, according to Abelard, are the ways in which it differs from certain particular disciplines.

Guided by the words of the 'auctoritates'[2], Abelard attributes logic to philosophy[3], which in turn is a 'scientia discernendi'.[4]

Having laid down that the 'genus' of logic lies in the 'scientia discernendi', its distinct theoretical character is removed from pure exercise and practical ability; and Abelard underlines this more than once.[5]

Let us now consider the definition of logic, which Abelard generally puts on the same footing as 'dialectica'.[6]

Logic or 'rationalis', which deals with 'de ratione argumentorum componenda'[7], is put beside 'speculative' or 'physical' philosophy, which investigates the nature and cause of things[8], and 'moralis' or 'ethica', the so-called standards of life.[9] It is thus defined as 'ratio disserendi' or 'diligens ratio disserendi' on the guidance of statements by the authorities.[10] For Abelard this is a 'discretio argumentandi', by which expression he insists on the distinction between logic and pure ability to discourse, since its basic character establishes the truth or untruth of the discourse (or 'argumentatio').[11] Logic is therefore the general and fundamental method in any investigation, because it is the basis of all the rules for any type of scientific or true discourse. Its formal character is emphasised in this way. And not only this: it can also be 'instrumentum sui', which brings to light its metalinguistic aspect. This point, to my knowledge, is an original Abelardian notation with regard to Boetius.

Abelard takes the principal division into 'scientia inveniendi' and 'scientia dijudicandi'[12], from Boetius, underlining the importance of the second which is aimed at the study of 'regulae certae', which establish the criterion of truth for a discourse.[13]

One can already anticipate, with Abelard, the two basic elements which make an 'argumentatio' true: the 'dispositio terminorum' and the 'natura rerum'.[14] Considering the first or the second, indestructible standards reinforcing any discourse will be established. We can note from now on that the first is the syntactical element, around the discourse itself, while the second must on no account be confused with the 'res', pure and simple.[15]

Having established that the end of logic is the construction of the true or scientific discourse[16], Abelard is aided in arranging the whole logical 'corpus' which is familiar to him, in accordance with an arrangement suggested by the composition of the 'argumentatio': we shall pass from an examination of the nouns and propositions to the 'inventio' of the 'argumentationes' and their 'confirmatio'.[17]

The nature of logic will be clearer if we consider first and foremost its differences from metaphysics, a distinction that is required by the particular condition of the discussions and polemics of the time on the nature of universals.

In this context there is a very significant and exhaustive passage in *Dialectica*.[18] Here there is a distinction between the two investigations and the relation between them is also established. With regard to the first point, logic and metaphysics are different because their definitions are different: one is concerned with the 'impositio vocum'[19] inasmuch as this is the operation whereby what is proposed by a noun or by an 'oratio' is established; the other, as is shown by other hints, is concerned with the 'res' and their properties[20], and in the case of an 'enunciato' is concerned with the 'natura rei' and the 'adaequatio' of the discourse to this.

The relation between logic and metaphysics is a result of the need for integration of the two studies: "Est autem alterius consideratio alteri necessaria."[21]

To have a perfect understanding of the meanings, an 'investigatio rerum naturae' will be vital to the person concerned with logic; in fact, as we shall see, the 'significatio intellectuum', as distinct from the 'significatio rerum'[22], is based and legitimised by a special real structure.[23] By consideration of the results of metaphysical studies, the 'intentio' of the dialectician "referenda est ad logicam".[24]

The debt, and the limits of this debt, which logic owes to metaphysics are clearly outlined in the statement: "Logica autem... res...non propter se, sed propter nomina tractat."[25]

By these statements Abelard's preoccupation with the real basis of the discourse is made quite evident; the attitude, which we shall come across in numerous other passages[26], is presented under two aspects: on the one hand the demand to separate the study of the properties of and relations between things from logical inquiry, on the other the implicit admission that these properties and relations are the basis of their nominal counterparts. As for the debt that 'physica' owes to logic, we have seen how logic – as the whole complex of rules for any type of discourse – is the general methodology of 'physica' as well, as it is for any other scientific investigation.[27]

One can thus see in Abelard a reciprocal conditioning of the two disciplines. The most interesting side of the logic-metaphysics relation is still, in my opinion, in the need for determined investigations (e.g. into universals) to remain within the limits of logic and not to become studies of a metaphysical nature as they might if the investigation was more into the 'natura rerum' than into the 'proprietas sermonum'[28] (which is then the 'natura rerum' not 'propter se' but 'propter nomina'). This is at once the consequence and the reason for which Abelard proceeds with this differentiation.

Metaphysics presents itself in this way as a science of essences, defined as a study of reality, while logic, the aim of which is the study of the validity of discourses, is only indirectly an inquiry into the real. As we have seen, Abelard recognises in the latter a formal character: respecting certain rules of 'calculus' one can affirm the correctness of certain reasonings without having recourse to the examination of the 'res'.[29] Nonetheless even for the construction of that perfect alignment of propositions which is the syllogism, the preliminary inquiry by logic into the property of things signified by nouns was necessary, with the result that Abelard is aware of the need to specify the sense in which the 'nomen' is taken in the 'argumentatio'. By this last aspect logic could be defined, in the Palatine Master's texts, as a 'discourse on reality', while metaphysics is a 'discourse of the real'.

Another distinction made and emphasised by Abelard is that between logic and inner discourse. This derives from the definition of logic as 'ratio disserendi'; with this expression Abelard excluded the formulation of unexpressed thoughts from logic and indicated that logic consists only in the sphere of uttered discourses and in the communication of propositions.

In this respect a passage from *Super Topica Glossae* in *Ingredientibus* seems to me to be exhaustive. Here the sphere of logic is clearly established, as is the criterion for distinguishing a logical phenomenon from one that might belong to gnoseology and unexpressed thought: this criterion is the 'altercatio' between men who are looking not for the truth 'realis', but the truth of the propositions they put forward.[30] This differs from the inner 'perscrutatio' in every man who inquires by himself and wants to establish what 'in re' corresponds to a concept of his.

It seems to me that Abelard here reaches his greatest rigour in defining the task of logic and in omitting and separating alien complications from its ambit: indeed, this rigour, though in evidence in other places[31], is almost isolated, or at least remains the most evident manifestation of the need to give logical inquiry complete autonomy. In fact, in his investigation on the meaning of universal nouns for example[32], Abelard unites the two types of inquiry, logic and gnoseology, with the help of the Aristotelian metaphysical conception: the result is the doctrine of abstraction.[33]

Having established the need to avoid metaphysical and gnoseological complications in dialectic research, one can see the need to distinguish it from other inquiries which also concern the discourse.

And above all from rhetoric, to which logic might seem too close, when one underlines its aspect of 'contentio ratiocinantium'.[34] It seems to me that in this respect Abelard's action pivots round two points, which are moreover interconnected:

(a) First of all, Abelard has more than once made the distinction between logic and mere practical ability in the rhetorician, who finds persuasive arguments suitable to be connected with the discoursive tissue[35], and he singled out the theoretical character of dialectic in its 'ratio' or awareness of assuming a strict criterion to construct and judge a discourse; a criterion which is never psychological[36];

(b) in addition Abelard aften reveals that the concept of 'argumentatio' the construction of which is presented as the purpose of logical inquiry, is quite different from the 'argumentatio' of the orator, constructed with a particular end in view, which he has in mind. The 'argumentatio' is the true discourse as an instrument of 'scientia'[37]; one can reach the truth of the 'argumentatio' by the perfection of 'complexio' of the discourse, or, if an imperfect 'complexio' is encountered, by recourse to the 'natura rerum' or 'terminorum'.[38] In any case the concatenation of the arguments is necessary.[39]

Abelard not only separates the study of probable arguments from the inquiry of the logician[40], but also tries to establish for this type of argument a criterion which is in a certain sense more determinable than the psychological criterion.[41] Logic is thus distinct from rhetoric because its method and its end are different.[42]

And one can trace this from the method by which Abelard conducts his investigation – from his examination of the 'nomen' to the 'dijudicatio' of an 'argumentatio' –, aiming at isolating a rigorous and certain legitimising criterion for every type of expression, and separating the subjective and psychological aspects to which an expressive phenomenon can be linked. Examples of this attitude are Abelard's tendency to lay down the meaning of a noun as a single, unitary and definite concept, avoiding subjective and transitory interpretations due to the 'nominatio' of a 'dictio'[43]; likewise his exclusion of the 'intellectus' as meanings of proposi-

tions inasmuch as they are unsteady and changeable[44]; his definition of the truth of an 'argumentatio' as its necessity, independent
of any subjective and thus rhetoristic interpretation.[45] The Abelardian procedure in the first two cases makes nouns and propositions
safe elements which are suited to be part of syllogistic and topical
calculation precisely because of the severity and unity of their
value when stripped of indeterminateness; in the third case Abelard
shows a tendency to study those 'regulae certae', within the discourse itself, which organise and establish the cardinal points of the
'collocutio', by laying down a definite systemisation for the 'argumentatio'.

The frequent references made by the Palatine Master in his
logical works to the grammatical construction of the discourse and
to the grammatical form of the terms[46] and the signs, in some
writings which point to his own *Grammatica*, require that one
tries to understand what, for Abelard, was the concept of 'grammatica' as distinct from 'logica' and the meaning that the consideration of the grammatical plane can have had for Abelard in his
dialectic inquiry.

A first brief but plain distinction between the two disciplines
emerges in *Ingredientibus* with regard to the concepts of 'constructio' and 'praedicatio'.[47] The first involves grammatical concepts, the second 'dialectic' or logical concepts. While the 'constructio' is a 'coniunctio' that requires the completeness of the 'sententia'
and the agreement of determined terms with determined termina-
tions, logic, with the end of an exact 'praedicatio' is concerned not
only with these elements but also with the truth of the statement.
This is indicated by Abelard, in this instance, by the 'demonstratio'
of a real state or nature.

Although this starting-point clarifies many future Abelardian
attitudes[48], one still has to consider that it is susceptible to varia-
tions: we shall see how, in more than one place, Abelard removes
himself from the theory of the 'adaequatio'.[49]

Dialectica reaffirms that it is the problem of meaning (and truth)
to distinguish between logical and grammatical inquiry.[50]

Another illuminating passage appears in the *Super Topica*

Glossae.[51] Abelard refers to the 'sententia' of the "praeceptor noster Willelmus", who attributed two 'sensus' to every proposition: a grammatical and a dialectical. Grammarians would in fact contemplate a single 'copulatio' in 'essentia', while logicians would be concerned with the 'praedicatio secundum inhaerentiam' and would successively investigate various types of this: "inhaerentia ut genus vel accidens...", or rather, "inhaerentia essentiae vel adiacentiae".

This 'sententia' seems to attribute to every proposition a dual value: according to the interpretation of grammarians, the 'nominata' of terms are the same thing; for dialecticians these are inherently interrelated. A similar 'coniunctio' would be set up, therefore, on two different relations of terms.[52] Abelard does not accept this view: "Nolumus autem unquam in constructionibus alium sensum dialectici, alium attendant grammatici."[53] Logic and grammar are two 'scientiae' – he says – which treat the same argument by using different terminologies: for a grammarian there will be the 'transitive' and 'intransitive copulatio'; for a dialectician the 'praedicatio secundum inhaerentiam' and the varying types of this.[54]

The sense of construction is identical and the value of the 'enunciatio' is the same; only the 'verba' used are different, because the purpose proposed in the two disciplines is different, if one recalls the other Abelardian passage.

Abelard's proposal thus aims at eliminating the difference between the two values that the same 'propositio' would possess, according to Willelmus, and at transforming it into a difference between two methods of inquiry, the grammatical concerning the 'coniunctio', and the logical that applies to the 'praedicatio' and thus, in most cases, to a 'res-nomen' relation.

It is thus only for 'scientia dialectica' that Abelard claims the task of establishing and judging the rules of the construction of a proposition with reference to its meaning, while it is to grammar, once again, that the agreement between terms which can be united transitively or intransitively is due.

There is another passage in the *Super Topica*[55] that regards the logic-grammar relation. Abelard here separates grammar and rhetoric from philosophy, of which logic on the other hand is a 'species', and he refuses to accept the proposal of those who consider grammar and rhetoric as parts of logic. With this statement as a basis we can establish that:

(a) Since 'philosophia' is not any old science, but is distinct from the others because of the object which is fundamental and the method which is scientific and strict[56], philosophical logic will have these features, which one can single out firstly in the inquiry that it develops into the truth of the discourse, and secondly in the 'ratio' that, unlike rhetoric, constitutes its instrument of exploration. Grammar, on the other hand, not being philosophy, certainly does not have the first, at least, of these features: it is a 'scientia'[57], the object of which is not the construction of the true discourse, but only a certain systemisation of the discourse. As for its method, this might be rational, like the method of logic, given the scientificity of grammar; Abelard lays down nothing in this respect and merely notes the difference in the object of inquiry.

(b) There is an interesting allusion to those who subordinate grammar, and rhetoric, to logic, even if it is practically impossible to pick them out. In this way logic would simply become the science that is generically concerned with the discourse and the inquiry into the rules that govern it, or the study of a persuasive argument, would harbour its solution.[58]

It thus seems possible to see in the Abelardian procedure a dual attitude: on one side he introduces, together with the traditional 'auctoritates' in logic, Priscian and his *Institutiones grammaticae* and sees as the basic element of an 'oratio', on which to carry out dialectic investigation, the 'constructio' of the same, or rather the 'competens coniunctio' of the 'dictiones' that transforms simple 'collectiones' of words into statements.[59] This 'constructio' is a systemisation that belongs to grammar. On the other side he not only distinguishes the two inquiries, but attributes greater dignity to dialectic 'inquisitio' as a study of the criterion of truth for the discourse. He is aware how insufficient it is at times to see the consideration of grammatical laws – understood in the common meaning – as supporting the syntax of scientific discourse. Grammar is not enough to assure the language of 'scientia' that rigorous unequivocability that is the preliminary of the inquiry of logic: discourses which show serious ambiguities are organised by pure grammatical rules.[60]

And again: conducting his own observations on the 'enuntiationes impersonales', guided by Priscian, he tends to resolve every type of grammatically impersonal proposition in a logically personal formula, in which the 'copulatio' or the 'remotio' are made in a way which is complete.[61] There would, in this way, be a mere grammatical difference but, logically, a perfect equivalence between the two types of 'enuntiationes'.

Arnold insisted on the first aspect of the Abelardian attitude, underlining how the Palatine Master bases his own logical thought on a grammatical conception of the expression.[62] It seems to me that an excessive insistence only on this side of the Abelardian procedure (an aspect which, as we have seen, is certainly present) leads to the affirmation of a generic Abelardian interest for the 'scientia grammatica' rather than to the consideration of the special meaning of the use which Abelard makes of grammatical rules in dialectic inquiry. 'Grammatica' in fact supplies Abelard with well-defined rules by which to construct the discourse, on the semantic function of which he then begins the real logical inquiry. As the language which Abelard examines is natural[63], the syntax by which it is to be ordered can only be provided by 'grammatica' in conversational language. Scientific language should spring, for Abelard, from investigation that the 'dialecticus' carries out on conversational language, which was still Latin in his day, constructed according to the grammatical rules which were, for the most part, suggested to him by Priscian. These rules, furthermore, revealed themselves to be inadequate, which means that the common language which is too frequently equivocable is an inadequate instrument of 'scientia'.

This is a good moment to return to that 'defence of logic' which will throw more light on Abelard's conception of and interest in this discipline.[64]

Given the position that this occupies in the plane of his studies, the defence of this discipline in fact becomes a self-defence. The accusation of Abelard's opponents and the foes of logic is based on two points: on the one hand it is alien to faith, and on the other it can harm it by its arguments.

Abelard's defence rests on one basic point: logic is a 'scientia'.[65] That an art[66], like the military art for example, can be harmful to the exercise of faith is understandable and admissible; the 'scientia', however – given the 'ratio' of its method and the dignity of the object ('veritatis rerum comprehensio') – can only derive from 'sapientia', like faith.

The term 'sapientia' seems to be used by Abelard in the original meaning of wisdom: in this way it conserves a breadth of meaning that allows it to embrace 'scientia' and 'fides'. 'Sapientia', we can say, is the possession of 'veritas': now both 'cognitio' or 'scientia' and faith aim at truth, which is good.[67] The desire to 'scire', or rather to know the truth, can never be an evil, even when one wants to know something which, inasfar as it is the object of an 'agere' is evil, like sin[68]: "ad actum referenda est malitia".[69]

From this one can deduce the superiority of the 'scientia discernendi' over the 'scientia agendi', as well as the definitive denial of the accusation made against logic.

This is not enough for Abelard: not only should logic be acquitted from 'calumnia', but it should also be attributed with that 'principatum' that competes with it in other 'scientiae'.[70] This preeminent position comes to it from its character of 'discretio veritatis seu falsitatis' of every type of discourse, which, in this way, must be constructed according to the dialectic rules to which it must be subject. This means that logic, as we have discovered, is the general method of all science.[71]

From this stems the necessity of not omitting to consider the fixed rules of 'dialectica' in a theological 'quaestio' as well, such as on the Trinity.[72]

Just as preaching the term 'Deus' – Father, Son, and Holy Ghost – does not create more Gods, because the term 'Deus' designates the same substance, so in preaching 'homo' of single individuals one must bear in mind that this term is also applied to a single substance.[73] Abelard nevertheless realises that there is not a perfect correspondence between the two cases under consideration[74], and he restricts himself to suggesting this 'argumentatio' by an initial and immediate 'impugnatio' of the false belief in the Trinity.[75]

The defence of logic closes with the confirmed statement that this discipline has a theoretical quality: one can inscribe in it not those who are endowed with a simple ability to discourse, but those who have 'ingenium', an indispensable quality in the application to 'scientia'.[76]

REFERENCES

[1] D., p. 469–71 (20).

[2] G.G., pp. 1 (7ff.), 505 (6ff).

[3] Together with Boetius, Abelard calls logic an instrument and integral part of philosophy (G.G., p. 1 (11–25).

[4] G.L., p. 209 (13); G.G., p. 506 (4).

[5] G.G., pp. 507 (4–13), 209 (34)–210 (21).

[6] G.G., p. 1 (10); D., pp. 3–36; G.G., p. 506 (21–2). As for Dialectica, the title itself shows that Abelard takes this term to be the equivalent of logic; indeed, in this text one comes across 'dialectica' more frequently than 'logic' (see D., p. 470 (4–6). One notices an important change in the introduction to the Super topica of Ingredientibus, in which Abelard makes a distinction between logic and dialectic; in fact he attributes a more comprehensive rôle to the former, while the second is rather only a part of logic which is concerned with probable and not necessary arguments (G.L., pp. 205 (16), 214 (14–21), and 292 (18)). The 'dialecticus' is accordingly linked with the 'orator'. (G.L., p. 315 (15)). This change would be incomprehensible, considering that there are two contrasting statements in Ingredientibus itself, if one did not take heed of the Boetian text on which Abelard is working. The statement by Boetius himself unites two traditions relating to the definition of 'dialectica'; the first comes from Aristotle who calls 'dialectica' that discipline concerned with probable arguments; the discipline of the Topici, in which the arguments are taken as probable or rather persuasive (Boetius, P.L., pp. LXIV, 1047). The 'dialecticus' is thus close to the 'orator' and its distinction from philosophy which deals with apodictic or demonstrative arguments (Boetius, P.L., pp. LXIV, 1182). Abelard too knows that this conception is Aristotelian (G.L., p. 211 (38–40). The second accepted meaning of 'dialectica' comes to Boetius from the Stoics who called any 'ars disserendi' in this way. Given that the Stoics knew only the 'iudicatio' and did not know the 'inventio' (Boetius, P.L., pp. LXIV, 1047), that is the part nearer to rhetoric, one can conclude that by 'dialectica' they meant the 'inquisitio' of the truth or untruth of the discourse that Abelard presents in Dialectica (D., p. 145 (10–1). In conclusion one can say that: (a)

when Abelard takes 'dialectica' and 'logica' as the equivalent of one another, he does so under the influence of the Stoic tradition which came to him through Boetius, contaminated by the Ciceronian and Boetian conception, which thus enables him to accept both the 'scientia inveniendi' and the 'scientia dijudicandi' in logic or dialectic (*G.G.*, pp. 506 (21), 507 (26)); (b) when 'logica' is distinct from 'dialectica', it is the Aristotelian conception, with the help of Boetius, which Abelard more particularly has in mind. In fact Abelard distinguishes between logic and dialectic precisely in the text in which Boetius had made the same distinction (*G.L.*, pp. 205 (16) and 214 (21); Boetius, *P.L.*, pp. LXIV, 1182). At all events, Boetius had distinguished between these two disciplines in the comment *Super Porphirium* as well (*P.L.*, pp. LXIV, 13), while in both the comments on the *Isagoge*, in which he tackles the problem, Abelard puts logic and dialectic in common (*G.G.*, pp. 3 (4–34) and 506 (21)), and by quoting the *Super Topica Ciceronis* of Boetius comes not to accept the distinction between logic and dialectic that Boetius had suggested to him (Boetius, *P.L.*, pp. LXIV, 1047ff.; *G.G.*, p. 3 (34)), a difference that he accepts elsewhere however (*G.L.*, p. 214 (15)). In the note *Quod antiquitus*, which Octavian published as an 'unpublished pamphlet of Abelard' (*Testi medievali inediti*, Florence 1933), 'logica' and 'dialectica' are used indifferently (see *op.cit.*, pp. 106–7).

7   *G.G.*, p. 1 (10).

8   *G.G.*, pp. 1 (8–9), 506 (10).

9   *G.G.*, pp. 1 (9), 506 (20).

10   *G.G.*, p. 506 (24–6); *G.L.*, p. 209 (15–22).

11   *G.G.*, p. 506 (25–8). We have already seen how the 'genus' of logic is to be seen in the 'scientia disserendi' (*G.G.*, p. 505, (6ff.); *G.L.*, p. 209 (12)). Incidentally, Abelard has underlined the rigorous and theoretical character of logical inquiry both in the term 'ratio' and in the term 'discretio'. The attribute of 'ars' in *Dialectica* seems to be contrary to this type of characterisation (*D.*, pp. 153 (1), 270 (28)). With this one would in fact tend to underline the practical (rhetorical) aspect of dialectic; otherwise the term 'ars' does not seem to have as precise a meaning if Cicero was already indicating the sciences by 'artes optimae'. This, however, shows the accepted meaning in which this term was used, in the Middle Ages, in the expression 'artes liberales'. See the corresponding passage in the note *Quod antiquitus* (Octavian, *op.cit.*, p. 108), where the theoretical nature of logic is underlined.

12   *G.G.*, pp. 3 (33ff.), 507 (14–26); *G.L.*, p. 209 (22ff.).

13   *G.G.*, pp. 2 (1ff.), 507 (27ff.).

14   *G.G.*, pp. 508 (11–5), 2 (3 and 4).

15   *G.G.*, p. 46 (2–3).

16   This point is continually confirmed in *Dialectica*: *D.*, pp. 121 (6), 278 (17), 152 (28).

17   *G.G.*, pp. 2 (8ff.), 508 (32ff.), 3 (11–4), 510 (14–6).

18   *D.*, pp. 286 (31), 287 (5).

19   *D.*, p. 114 (25).

20   *D.*, pp. 65 (19), 96 (12), 217 (2).

21   *D.*, p. 286 (35).

22   See as from now the passage *G.G.*, p. 309 for the distinction between 'significatio rerum' and 'significatio intellectuum'.

23 The most significant passage in this respect is that concerning the study of the 'causa communis' validifying the 'intellectus' of universal nouns. *G.G.*, p. 23 (20–4).

24 *D.*, pp. 287 (1), 166 (9): "At vero magis praedicationem secundum verba propositionis quam secundum rei existentiam nostrum est attendere qui logicae deservimus..."

25 *D.*, p. 99 (5–6). Similar statements are found in *D.*, pp. 73 (3–5) and 286 (38). See Octavian (*op.cit.*, p. 108: "Oportet eum [logicum] esse discretum in distinctione omnium argumentorum exposita tantum ei natura seu rerum seu vocum..."

26 E.g., *G.G.*, p. 537 (7–10).

27 See p. 13.

28 *G.G.*, pp. 514 (32), 515 (9).

29 *D.*, pp. 233 (d), 253 (29), 254 (1).

30 *G.L.*, p. 305 (12ff.).

31 As, for example, in the inquiry into the "significans verum vel falsum" of a proposition. See *G.G.*, pp. 365–6. See also *G.L.*, p. 296 (16–23), where the logic-gnoseology distinction is confirmed.

32 *G.G.*, p. 18ff.

33 Which, as we shall see, nonetheless shows a significative originality in respect of Aristotle's metaphysical conception.

34 *G.L.*, p. 305 (16). Prantl, on the contrary, holds that Abelard's basic attitude is that of the rhetorician, believing that by making the 'argumentatio' the end of logic he reveals a practical interest in the discourse. The Abelardian attitude, aimed at specifying 'veritas' as the basic nature of the dialectic 'argumentatio' is even more notable if one considers that logic, at the time of the Palatine Master, was not immune from the influx of rhetoric which, by putting itself up as the end of persuasive discourse, turned its attention to the psychological values of expression. We can trace this back from two precious pieces of evidence provided by Abelard when he refers to the position of those who resolved logic in rhetoric and grammar (*G.L.*, p. 290 (2–16)), and the 'sententia' of the 'Magister' who said "probabile cum vero convenire" (*D.*, pp. 271–2). The influx of rhetoric appears on the contrary to be present only in Abelardian terminology and not in his conception of 'logica'. On superficial examination this may lead to the statement of a fundamental rhetorical spirit in Abelard. Abelard thus calls 'altercatio' or 'contentio ratiocinantium' the criterion that distinguishes logic from inner discourse and unexpressed thought, and means by 'significare' 'constituere intellectum auditoris', where, however, the accepted meaning, 'strictior', in which the term 'intellectus' is used ('intellectus sanus') prevents us from considering this expression as a sign of a rhetorical attitude.

35 *G.G.*, p. 507 (4–13); *G.L.*, pp. 209 (34), 210 (21).

36 *G.G.*, p. 508 (11–5); *G.L.*, p. 2 (3–4).

37 *D.*, p. 153 (1–3; 8–11).

38 *D.*, p. 255–7.

39 *G.L.*, p. 309 (13–7).

40 *D.*, p. 271–2.

41 *G.L.*, pp. 309 (16ff.)–31; *D.*, p. 277 (16ff.). See also the example of 'locus probabile' in *D.*, p. 338.

42 The disinterest that Abelard shows in his logical inquiry for rhetorical

phenomena is quite clear in a remark belonging to the comment on *De Inter-pretatione* (*G.G.*, pp. 121–2). With Boetius he distinguishes two origins of the 'aequivicatio': the 'consilium' and the case in which the noun is used to designate a concept which is not its own, 'ornatus gratia'. This reason is ephemeral and carries no weight in a dialectic study.

[43] *D.*, pp. 112–3.

[44] *G.G.*, p. 366 and *D.*, pp. 154–5.

[45] *D.*, p. 271 (27).

[46] The passage in *D.*, p. 124 (27–9) is interesting, where Abelard marries the significative type of property with two other ambits as a viewpoint from which to see the characteristics of a noun: one is the 'positio constructionis', the clearly grammatical element. See the passage *D.*, pp. 171–2, about the concordance 'in numero' of the subject and the verb. The Abelardian inquiry into 'dictiones indefinitae' is of interest, which, according to the Aristotelian-Boetian logical tradition was not considered part of the discourse. See *D.*, pp. 118ff. and *G.G.*, pp. 337ff.

[47] *G.G.*, p. 17 (12–28).

[48] Like the proposed solution to the problem of universals (*G.G.*, p. 19 (21ff.)) and the conception of categorical propositions (*D.*, p. 282 (30ff.).

[49] For example in the concept of 'dictum propositionis' (*G.G.*, p. 327 (20ff.)), in the inquiry into hypothetical cases (*D.*, p. 282 (30ff.)), in the examination of the syllogism (e.g. *D.*, p. 499 (30–2).

[50] *D.*, p. 121 (21ff.). In this passage the examination of the 'dictiones definitae' with regard to logic is affirmed, while that of the 'dictiones indefinitae' remains the task of grammar. In fact the 'dictiones definitae' link – more so than each other – the parts of the discourse and their meaning is not determining in a proposal of truth or untruth. Hereby Abelard partly corrects the initial position (*D.*, p. 118) and returns to the Aristotelian position which he already had in his *Ingredientibus* (*G.G.*, pp. 337–9).

[51] *G.L.*, pp. 271 (38), 274 (19).

[52] See in particular *G.L.*, p. 272.

[53] *G.L.*, p. 273 (37–9).

[54] See in particular *G.L.*, p. 274.

[55] *G.L.*, p. 290 (2–16).

[56] *G.G.*, p. 1 (5–7).

[57] *G.L.*, p. 274 (9).

[58] The difference between logical inquiry and grammatical inquiry is also evident in another passage of *Ingredientibus* where one can deduce that the light in which 'dialecticians' and 'grammarians' consider the discourse differs (*G.G.*, p. 384 (30ff.)).

[59] *G.G.*, pp. 364–5; *D.*, pp. 147–8.

[60] *D.*, p. 587 (30).

[61] *G.G.*, pp. 390–2. An analogous and more accentuated consideration of the logical plane with regard to the grammatical 'constructio' emerges from the passage *D.*, pp. 481 (32)–2 (4), where Abelard opposes Boetius, who considered the 'temporales' 'hypotheticae', because he did not find in them a 'conditio' or 'consecutio' by which the truth of the antecedent requires the truth of the consequent. In the 'temporales', Abelard observes, there is only a 'comitatio'

or a simultaneity of truth. Abelard does not therefore pay attention to the analogy of features with which 'temporales' and 'hypothetica naturalis' are presented in conversational language, but rather to the substantial difference between these two, reduced to pure logical formulae.

[62] Arnold, *Zur Geschichte der Suppositionstheorie*, Freiburg 1952, p. 65.

[63] At times Abelard shows, however, an accentuated disinterest for natural language, and resorts, as did Boetius, to the use of letters to indicate propositions which constitute accordingly the variable values of determined 'argumentationes' (*D.*, pp. 497, 499).

[64] *D.*, pp. 469–71 (20).

[65] *D.*, p. 469 (13–6).

[66] It is clear that the term 'ars' is taken in two different accepted meanings: one generic, whereby one can talk of 'ars dialectica', the other more determined, indicating the exercise of a profession or a determined type of action. In this sense one talks of 'ars militaris' as opposed to 'scientia'.

[67] *D.*, p. 469 (17–25).

[68] *D.*, p. 469 (23–5). Abelard retorts to his adversaries with the accusation of 'bad Christian'. If one in fact admits that 'scientia' is evil, "quomodo ipse quoque Deus malitia absolvi potest?".

[69] *D.*, p. 469 (33). This passage seems to me a precious integration to Abelard's views on ethics which it would be interesting to bear in mind in a reading of the *Scito te ipsum*.

[70] *D.*, p. 470 (4–6).

[71] Cf. the expression 'scientia scientiarum' (P. Ispano, *Summulae logicales*, Turin 1947, p. 1). and 'disciplina disciplinarum' of St. Augustine (Bréhier, *La filosofia del Medio Evo*, Turin, 1952, p. 171).

[72] *D.*, p. 470 (7–26).

[73] In the case of 'homo' one would rather expect the affirmation that this indicates a single 'natura', considering the observations of *Ingredientibus* (*G.G.*, pp. 19 (21)–20 (14)), but one must keep in mind both the need for an analogy between the two 'argumentationes', 'de Deo', and 'de homine', and the fact that 'substantia' does not always indicate an existence, but also a way of being, as in the Aristotelian-Abelardian accepted meaning of second substance.

[74] *D.*, p. 470 (24–6).

[75] It is interesting to note how Abelard's attitude in this passage is very like that of St. Anselm (Prantl, *op.cit.*, p. 144, note 319), when he reproaches Roscellin of having fallen into tritheism precisely because of his nominalistic conception of universals. Both Anselm and Abelard therefore connect these two views: Abelard, though, as we shall see, polemically distinguishing his conception of universals from the realistic conception, finds in the doctrine of the 'status' the element that enables him to combine in a similar way with Anselm with regard to the 'quaestio' on the Trinity and the 'quaestio' *sui generi*. Far from Roscellin in this, who, by pushing his refusal of realism to the limits, had inevitably and coherently to arrive at a tritheistic conception of the Trinity (Prantl, *op.cit.*, p. 146).

[76] *D.*, pp. 470 (27)–1 (10).

CHAPTER II

THE PROBLEM OF MEANING

Having established that the purpose of studying the criterion of truth of speech is logical inquiry, the need inevitably arises, for Abelard, to make a preliminary examination of the meaning of the elements that constitute an 'oratio'.[1] It has in fact been clearly stated that the task of logic is the construction of a 'propositio vera' and that the study of the complex element of the expression justifies and requires the study of the atomic elements of which it is composed.[2] The 'significatio' thus comes to be one of the fundamental factors of dialectic inquiry; though not the purpose of this latter, it is nonetheless a vital introduction to the problem of truth.[3]

Abelard himself says that the noun and the verb are privileged parts of a proposition because of the 'perfectio' of their 'significatio'.[4] In what does the 'perfectio' consist?

To establish the range of the term 'significatio', it helps to return through the definitions and observations, concerning this important point, which Abelard imparted in the comments on the *Isagoge*, the *Categorie* and *De Interpretatione*, as far back as the early discriminative reason for which two values are attributed to the term 'significare': the one logical, the other generic, yet ascientific.

If 'significativum' were simply understood as everything that is 'nota' of something other than itself, any 'vox' would be significative of the presence of this being inasmuch as it is a sound emitted by a living being.

In two passages in the *Glosse Letterali* and the *Dialectica*[5], Abelard shows that he is aware that this would lead to an initial lack of distinction where the 'voces' were concerned, and to the subsequent impossibility of arriving at the definition of 'nomen' from that of 'vox significata'.[6]

Even before embarking on the study of the Aristotelian Boetian expression 'ad placitum', Abelard therefore considers it necessary to point out that 'significativum' should be taken as indicating the potentiality of an articulated sound to be referred not only to the concept of the presence of the 'prolator' but also to the other concept that this 'prolator' has wanted to express.

And at this point we are already at the heart of the question: on the one hand it is clear that 'significare' is 'generare' or 'constituere', a concept[7] or even an intellective action of comprehension in the listener or reader[8]; on the other hand it is evident that, in order to make this exchange of 'intellectus' by means of 'voces' possible, a criterion of agreement is involved, which is what Abelard means by the 'institutio'.[9]

Let us look at the first point.

In the texts with which we are familiar, Abelard gives many definitions of 'significare' and makes frequent observations about the significative function of a term.[10] It is possible to divide these definitions into two groups: to the first belong those referring to the 'significatio de rebus'; to the second those referring to the 'significatio de intellectibus'. The clearest distinction is to be found in the comment on the *Categorie* of the *Ingredientibus*.[11]

Now, if the signification 'de intellectibus' is the first and principal semantic function of a noun and the most important in order of the 'causa impositionis', because a noun is formed precisely "ut intellectus constituet", but 'naturaliter' nonetheless, this is in accordance with the chronological development of the process of 'inventio', the signification 'de rebus' is 'prior'. The plan of the formative process of a noun, according to Abelard, results as: (1) a consideration of the 'natura rei' that motivates the 'inventio' of a noun with the necessity that this suggests to it; (2) 'impositio' of the noun whereby this is delegated to 'constituere intellectum'.

Whence one can see that the significative is the opposite of the inventive process.[12]

At this point we know that a noun uttered can refer to, or, as a result of this and other passages[13], mean, either a 'res', consideration of which has motivated the formation of the noun itself, or an 'intellectus'[14], which is precisely what the 'prolator' has to communicate to the others.

From the standpoint of this distinction, it thus seems that there is a large gap separating the two functions that a noun can have, the one referring to the world of reality, the other to the intellectual order.

But Abelard minimizes this difference by two statements: (a) the intellectual plane is the necessary intermediary, even when the function for which a term is formed to designate things is subject to examination[15]; (b) on the other hand if the world of 'res', in the case of the 'significatio rerum' is, by concept, the particular designation of the noun, it is certainly not absent or useless in the case of the 'significatio intellectuum'. In fact, inasmuch as in a 'significatio' of this type the 'intellectus' is the sole purpose for using a determined noun, this 'intellectus' must nevertheless rely on a particular real structure which relates to it within certain limits if it is not to be 'cassus' or futile (and subsequently unusable for 'scientia').[16]

'Significatio rerum' and 'significatio intellectuum' are therefore two functions of one term, differing more by the intensity of their action than by the quality of direction[17]: the first aims at indicating the real order and requires that the intellect in this case is responsible for reflecting the 'res' clearly; the purpose of the second is to communicate concepts which, in order to be valid, should at least draw the proper legitimization from the structure of the 'res', even if they do not retrace it.

We have already seen how Abelard shows quite clearly that the 'significatio de intellectibus' is more important for a logical inquiry. He confirms this in several places[18] and confirms this position with the 'significatio intellectum' as the constant aim of particular inquiries.[19]

Abelard singles out three reasons which make the 'significatio intellectus' important in a logical study:

(1) the 'intellectus' seems to be the most constant criterion to distinguish the various parts of speech, while an inquiry based on the 'significatio rerum' would lead to a complete lack of distinction, e.g. between adjective and substantive[20];

(2) the 'intellectus' of propositions consists of the 'intellectus' of their parts, while one cannot say that the 'res subiectae' of the

noun and the verb give rise to a 'res' of the proposition, given that this "nullam habeat rem subiectam"[21];

(3) the meaning 'intellectuum' persists even if things disappear.[22]

We find a further clarification in this direction in the text of the *Dialectica*, from which it emerges that not only is the 'significatio intellectuum' a privileged 'significatio', but it is also the only legitimate semantic function of a noun, the only function which a dialectician should bear in mind in examining speech.

The passage appears in *De Significatione*: Abelard intervenes in a polemic between Garmundus and *Magister V*[23] and falls in with the former because he holds to 'ratio, while the latter bases himself on authority.

The 'quaestio' hinges on what is meant by a noun, and by affirming that 'significare' is an 'intellectum generare' Abelard states that it is inadmissible that "de quo in sententia eius non agitur" is also meant. A noun does not signify things named, because of which it has been imposed, but simply the concept for which it is supposed[24]: "manifestum est eos [= Garmundus] velle vocabula non omnia significare quae nominant sed ea tantum quae definite designant, ut animal substantium animatam sensibilem...".[25]

In this passage the concept of 'impositio'[26] is introduced side by side with that of 'significatio', that is the concept of the choice of a 'vox' to designate something on behalf of men. The fundamentality of the creative act (the 'ad placitum' of Aristotle and Boetius) is frequently underlined by Abelard. This is so in the whole passage of *Nostrorum*[27], where Abelard clearly indicates that the being created or forced to have a meaning – differing from other natural sounds – is a necessary feature of a preachable noun (that is, it can be used in a 'propositio' and thus in a refined logical 'argumentatio'.

The human 'impositio' of a term is a conventional act[28]; nevertheless if the choice of the 'vox' as a 'nota' is arbitrary, one aspect of the 'impositio' is linked to the structure of things.

The first 'inventor' to impose expressions, saw right into the nature of reality according to Abelard[29], with the result that the ties linking determined groups of nouns can be derived from real ties[30], and that likewise the 'impositio' of a term is conditioned by the consideration of things whose indication is the effective cause of the 'impositio' itself.

Returning to the passage in *Dialectica*, which seems clearer to us now, we can see how Abelard affirms that every 'impositio' is motivated by the 'res', which constitute the original cause of the 'inventio' and that they will be the object of a secondary function of the expression: the 'appellatio' or 'nominatio'. This function, which Abelard underclasses with respect to the 'significatio' properly speaking and which he does not take into account in his dialectic examination of terms[31], is the function which has elsewhere been called 'significatio rerum' and already declared as secondary.[32]

One thus comes to isolate the concept of real 'significatio' as the potentiality of a term to solicit an 'intellectus'; this function of the expression remains independent of any other faculty of 'appellare' those 'res' which have been the original reason for the 'impositio' of the term itself.

The problem arises with regard to the relation between the significative and the nominative plane, that is to say, given that the latter is perfectly determined by the 'impositio', one is arguing whether every 'impositio' leads to a 'significatio'.

Opposed to resorting to the grammatical plane, according to which every expression means everything that it names and because of which it has been imposed, Abelard, together with Garmundus, supports a more determined and precise criterion of 'significatio'. The accepted meaning of to mean being established in 'intellectum generare', we cannot attribute a function to 'significatio' which would exceed these limits: the meaning of a noun is exclusively that which is expressed in this noun.

In this way the 'significatio' is restricted with regard to the ambit of the 'impositio' which conditions it but does not determine it, and indicated clearly as the function whereby a noun designates a concept and nothing else. We can thus single out in the Abelardian conception of 'significare' two phases which are not chronological[33], but which are both at times present in the same text.

In the first Abelard recognises two significative functions in the noun: 'rerum' and 'intellectum', derived from the two aspects of the 'impositio' itself, the one directed at the 'propter hoc', that is at the consideration of existing things [34] which have to be indicated, the other at the 'ad hoc', or rather at the concept which the 'prolator' wants to convey.

In the second phase Abelard says that the 'significatio rei' which he indicates more exactly as 'appellatio' or 'nominatio' is irrelevant and therefore not legitimate, and it is only in the 'significatio intellectuum' that he recognises the character of 'significatio' which comes to be the designatory function of a single, unitary and well-defined 'conceptio'.[35]

The most immediately evident value of this Abelardian procedure is a basic tendency to bring together dialectic examination of the exclusive sphere of nouns and their meanings, the latter being in turn freed or rather separated by a direct encounter with the real.

If in fact the only real 'significatio' of this sort is that 'de intellectibus', one must search exclusively in the features of which the concepts are endowed [36] with the criterion of distinction between the various nouns, while in the case of the 'nominatio' it is the plane of the 'res' that has to endow the various nouns with different qualities.

We shall see how this is only one of the aspects of Abelard's attempt to render the relation of the discourse with the real less immediate: this incidentally was already made clear in the definition of 'logica'.

The most macroscopic case of this procedure towards a rupture of the unity of the Aristotelian-Boetian triad: 'res-intellectus-nomen' is, as we shall see, the doctrine of the universals, which is better examined separately because of the huge development that Abelard allots to his discussion of it.

There are numerous examples of the value of choosing the 'significatio intellectuum' as the criterion in a logical inquiry.[37] So as not to anticipate any part of the Abelardian doctrine of universals, one can instead examine a passage from the treatise *De Specie* belonging to the comment on the *Isagoge* of the *Ingredientibus*.

Abelard intervenes over the difference of opinion between Porphyrius and Boetius. The first in fact maintains that 'phoenix' is single, given that the Phoenix is unique; the second says the Phoenix is a species.[38] Abelard notes that Porphyrius holds to the 'actus continentiae', while Boetius looks 'ad naturam', and takes sides with this latter because he is greatly concerned with the cause 'impositionis', more so than with the host of actual things to which a noun refers.[39] He considers the expression 'hic phoenix' indicative of a singular, thanks to the discretionary action of the pronoun, while 'phoenix' is a species.

If the meaning of the noun derives its value and its nature from the plane of the 'res' which have motivated its 'inventio', clearly 'phoenix' would be individual just as Socrates is; but Abelard is concerned not so much with a comparison between the noun and reality as with the necessity of determining for each noun, with precision and invariability, a concept as its meaning: the noun will then be called singular or general by the type of 'conceptio'.

A noteworthy consequence of the separation of 'significatio' from 'nominatio' is that, in the use of a noun, subjective and transitory interpretations carry no weight, as would be the precise case if the 'nominatio' were taken as the criterion.[40] In this way the psychological criterion of whoever claims, in a logical inquiry, to want to consider that the meaning of a noun lies in the real temporary designations which, at the time, affect the end of the discourse in question, is declared illegitimate.

With psychologism and subjectivism, rhetoricism is separated from the field of logic: the Abelardian procedure instead guarantees the noun that unity of meaning which makes it fit to become a sure element of syllogistic and topical calculation.

One need not, however, stress the importance of the Abelardian attempt to liberate the world of discourse – in our case the noun – from a certain 'adaequatio' to the 'res'. This attitude, as we have seen, is certainly evident in the Palatine Master's texts, but it is less complete and definite than one might think on first examination.

The 'sanitas', 'perfectio', and 'dignitas' of the meaning clarify the limits of Abelard's procedure.

A clear definition of the features that make the 'significatio intellectuum' of a noun 'sana' is given in the comment on *De Interpretatione* of *Ingredientibus*.[41]

In this passage the discussion centres on the 'intellectus'.[42] The question, namely, is asked when the 'intelligere' solicited by hearing a noun should be considered valid or rather positively usable in a scientific proposition[43], or valueless, that is 'cassus'.

"Sanus est omnis intellectus…per quem attendimus uti res se habent"[44]; if everything emerges clearly when one talks of singular realities such as 'Socrates', the 'quaestio' with regard to general nouns arises instead.

Without looking ahead to the remarks that will be made on the Abelardian doctrine of universals, one can sum up, with Abelard himself, the two values that the proposition referred to earlier can have, depending on whether one is dealing with singular or universal nouns.

The 'intellectus' of the first *reproduces* the 'res'[45]; that of the second *is based* not on a 'res' or 'essentia' but on a structure of 'res'.[46]

Still in *Ingredientibus*, we find another clear-cut definition of the 'sanitas' of an 'intellectus'.[47]

When asked if names of non-existing things such as 'chimaera' and 'hircocervus' fall – because of the type of their meanings – into the category of 'substantia', he replies that, by 'significare', taking only a wide meaning of 'intellectus', one could say that 'chimaera' means 'substantia'. In fact this would only happen in the case when 'intellectus' indicates some conception of the mind, with no distinction between opinion 'cassa sine re' and 'conceptio sana'. He opts for the restricted meaning of 'intellectus' and thus of 'significatio', which requires that the concept contains a confirmation of the real order.

The names of 'non-existing things' will not therefore mean 'substantia'.

Numerous other passages indicate that Abelard accepts as 'significatio' only that which in some way re-becomes the real order.[48]

One very conspicuous exception is made, as we shall see, in a passage of *Nostrorum,* in which Abelard – under the pressure of the difficulties surrounding the argument in question – seems to extend the validity of the 'intelligere' beyond the limits of a certain 'adaequatio' to the real.[49]

Another feature that limits the process of freeing the noun from the world of 'res' is the 'perfectio significationis'. Among all the parts of the discourse, or rather among all the 'voces significativae', Abelard indicates various parts which are privileged compared to the others, because they are endowed with a determined completeness of meaning.

In his inquiry into prepositions and conjunctions, Abelard shows himself to be plainly opposed to basing – by these 'dictiones' – the 'significatio intellectuum' on the 'significatio rerum' and aims at acquiring another type of meaning freed from the appellative function that usually accompanies it and makes it legitimate.[50]

Having carried out this study of the noun and the verb[51], he calls them: "Quae quidem sola ex significationis privilegio inter partes orationis dialectici recipiunt."[52]

Having thus laid down that some 'dictiones' have a 'significatio de intellectibus', not based on the 'res' or on its structures, Abelard nonetheless says that these 'dictiones' are imperfectly significative. This confirms the fundamentality of a legitimisation by the real through the meaning.

Another very significant consideration in this respect occurs in the comment on the *Categorie* of *Ingredientibus.*[53]

Abelard says that special nouns, from the moment that "determinantius rem subiectam nominant ... melius et certius eam significant".

Coinciding with the appellative function, the meaning of singular nouns is precise and cannot be confused; it is thus 'dignior'.

Those 'dictiones' which base their meaning on reality thus have a greater 'dignitas'.[54]

REFERENCES

[1] *D.,* p. 121 (5–7).
[2] *G.G.,* pp. 111, 307 (20–3).
[3] The comments on the *Isagoge,* the *Categorie* and the greater part of the comments on *De Interpretatione* deal with the problem of the meaning of terms.

⁴ *D.*, p. 121 (4).

⁵ *G.L.*, p. 76; *D.*, p. 111 (13–6).

⁶ "...Omnis vox est significativa quia generat intellectum de suo prolatore in auditorem, id est facit signum auditori se esse prolatum ab aliquo animali ... significativum hoc modo est restringendum ad hoc ut sit differentia vocis in diffinitione nominis: significativum est generans intellectum auditori de aliqua re recepta praeter suum prolatorem..." (*G.L.*, p. 76 (13–7)).

⁷ *G.G.*, p. 136 (29).

⁸ *G.G.*, pp. 339 (20)–40 (6).

⁹ *G.G.*, p. 112 (40).

¹⁰ Abelard uses 'terminus' in the sense of 'meta': "Partes terminos, id est metas, nominamus..." (*D.*, p. 164 (6)).

¹¹ *G.G.*, p. 112 (29)–3 (3).

¹² Abelard uses the term 'causa impositionis' in two senses: the first that of 'causa comune oggettiva', or that aspect of things that legitimizes an 'impositio'; (see *G.G.*, p. 19 (15)); the second suggests instead "the end for which an imposition has come about" and is constituted by the 'intellectus' that a noun signifies (see *G.G.*, p. 112 (37–41).

¹³ *G.G.*, p. 307 (27).

¹⁴ It is vital in this respect to see what Abelard means by 'intellectus', which means that one must refer to his last gnoseological doctrine. The most exhaustive description is contained in the comment on *De Interpretatione* of the *Ingredientibus* (*G.G.*, pp. 312ff.). One can see how Abelard expounds his considerations by following those of Boetius (*G.G.*, pp. 313–6 passim), from which he takes and recomposes the fragments of Aristotle's conception, to which, through the same Boetius, he frequently appeals. From Priscian and Boetius Abelard also derives brief documentations on the Platonic conception of the cognoscitive faculties (*G.G.*, pp. 314 (14–24), 315 (26–8)), which he does not accept, however, and discards in favour of the Aristotelian assertions. A further source of the Abelardian exposition in respect of the cognoscitive process is indicated in the *Rhetorica ad Herennium* (*G.G.*, p. 314 (7–12)), in which fragments of the Stoic cognoscitive theory were possibly present (see Sikes, *Peter Abailard*, Oxford 1933, pp. 108–10).

It seems to me that the following points emerge from the Abelardian exposition: (a) the distinction between intellect on the one hand, and sense and imagination on the other, on a basis of the 'irrationality' of the last two (*G.G.*, p. 113 (16–7). It is clear in what these consist from the considerations which follow, from which it emerges that while sense and imagination, referring respectively to the physical 'res' and to an 'imago' or 'similitudo' of this, consider it simply in its appearance, the intellect looks more particularly at the 'natura' and 'proprietas' of the 'res' (*G.G.*, pp. 315–7 passim). The function of the intellect would therefore be to penetrate the inner structure of things, their 'ordo', which is why the intellect presents itself as the typical instrument of knowledge (*G.G.*, pp. 505–6); (b) the statement that these 'similitudines' are not the aim of the 'impositio vocum', which is rather inclined to the 'intellectus', that is the comprehension and designation of 'res' ('significatio intellectuum' and 'significatio rerum'). These 'figmenta' are nothing other than 'intersigna rerum' or instruments through which comprehension is achieved, when the things are not present

(*G.G.*, pp. 21 (21), 315 (14–6)). These are only required in cases such as this, however; in the case of the 'res' which should be 'intellecta' being present, the intellective 'actio' is, certainly in an intermediary capacity, directed at it. The limited use made by Abelard of the 'similitudo' that recurs only when the object to be recognized is absent considerably simplifies the process of the intellective activity.

Contrary, therefore, to what Sikes and Octavian draw one's notice to, it seems to me that the gnoseological position of Abelard is clearly distinct from what would be St. Thomas's doctrine of the 'species' (Octavian, *P. Abelardo*, pp. 132–6, and Sikes, *op.cit.* p. 107).

[15] *G.G.*, p. 307 (30).

[16] *G.G.*, pp. 18 (6–9, 22 (7–24), 23 (20–4).

[17] Both these run through the *res-intellectus-vox* triad that Abelard finds in Aristotle and Boetius, and which he extensively illustrates in the comment on *De Interpretatione* of the *Ingredientibus* (see *G.G.*, pp. 321–3, 74).

[18] See e.g. *G.G.*, pp. 309 (23), 112 (40), 115 (40).

[19] E.g.: in examining the meaning of universals (*G.G.*, pp. 27, 531), in the inquiry on univocality (see *D.*, p. 222), which is as it is only in respect of the unity of 'conceptio', leaving the multiplicity of the 'res' meant out of consideration. Abelard proceeds in this way in his examination of compound nouns (*G.G.*, pp. 341–2 and *D.*, pp. 115–6).

[20] *G.G.*, p. 308 (22–3).

[21] *G.G.*, p. 308 (34–40).

[22] *G.G.*, p. 309 (1–3); see *G.G.*, p. 30 (1–5).

[23] With regard to the *Magister V*, mentioned in *Dialectica*, De Rijk raises a question. He refuses to read – as does Cousin – 'Magister Willelmus', because, he says, the 'sententia' attributed to the 'Magister V' is quite removed from the realistic views of Guillaume ('Introduction', in *D.*, p. xx). He suggests that one reads 'Magister Ulgerius', who is never expressly mentioned in Abelard's works, but who, as De Rijk supposes, was his master at the St. Maurice school, before Abelard went to Paris. As for the agreement of 'sententia', referred to in *D.*, p. 112, with Ulgerius' position, De Rijk points to a passage in *Theologia Christiana* where a "magister…in Andegavensi pago magni nominis" is attributed with the opinion that would agree with the opinion referred to in *Dialectica*. According to the master mentioned in the *Theologia Christiana*, the nouns which are proper to creatures belong to God; in this way God is said to be just, strong and wise.

A point common to these theories and the theory of *Dialectica* is the indeterminateness and arbitrariness to which the significative phenomenon is subject. It seems to me, however, that in *D.*, pp. 112–3, Abelard very directly points to and reproaches the identification of the nominative with the significative plane: "velle vocabula…omnia significare quae nominant…".

Furthermore the name Ulgerius does not figure in the passage in question in the *Theologia* either; it is no more than fairly likely that he is being referred to.

The consideration of the nominative plane as determining the value of the meaning is attributed in *Nostrorum* to a certain 'Magister Vasletus' (*G.G.*, p. 544 (22–6)). He considered the nouns 'sol' and 'phoenix' to be singular, because, in defining their meaning, he was taking the ambit of the 'res nominatae' into account. The position of Vasletus is therefore analogous with that of 'Magister V' in *Dialectica*, and is the result of an identical viewpoint.

In the case of the passage in *Theologia Christiana* it is rather a question, in my opinion, of a vaguer analogy; here one of two possible attitudes to the theological discourse is in evidence, rather than a determined theory of the 'significatio'. I would therefore suggest that in the identification of 'Magister V' one should take into consideration the figure of Vasletus who is one of the few 'magistri' mentioned by Abelard, but one can likewise not be certain that Ulgerius was Abelard's master. De Rijk confirms his interpretation in *Logica modernorum*, Assen 1967, vol. I, part II, p. 190, n. 1.

24 *D.*, pp. 112–3.

25 See the passage in the comment on *De Interpretatione* (*G.G.*, p. 355) where Abelard makes the distinction between the 'propter hoc' or the consideration of the real plane that motivates the 'inventio' of the noun, and the 'ad hoc' or the plane of meaning and the final cause of the 'impositio'.

26 Either 'inventio' (*D.*, p. 118 (28)) or 'institutio' (*G.G.*, p. 522 (16)).

27 *G.G.*, p. 522 (11ff.).

28 *G.L.*, p. 74 (89); *G.G.*, p. 321 (10–6).

29 *G.G.*, p. 112 (34-5); *G.G.*, p. 567 (27ff.)

30 The example of the 'causa comunis' is valid for all in *G.G.*, p. 19 (21ff.); see also *G.L.*, p. 31 (19–30) and *G.G.*, p. 532 (3–8).

31 *G.G.*, pp. 22 and 29, for example.

32 *G.G.*, pp. 112 and 309.

33 What I call the first phase occurs in the comment of *Ingredientibus* on the *Isagoge*, in *Dialectica* and in *Nostrorum* (*G.G.*, p. 22 (2–4) and *D.*, pp. 112–3; *G.G.*, p. 525 (2)). The second attitude is visible, on the contrary, in the comments on *De Interpretatione* and the *Categorie* of *Ingredientibus* (*G.G.*, pp. 113 (26–33), 309 (14–5). Both attitudes occur in the comment of *Ingredientibus* on the *Isagoge* (*G.G.*, p. 29 (37)).

34 Note that the 'appellatio' in Abelard, given its metaphysics which are Aristotelian (*G.G.*, pp. 30 (9–13)), 515 (14), 518 (9)) is always and only to the individual 'res'.

35 There is a further and extremely clear confirmation of this attitude in *Dialectica* with regard to the 'aequivoci' nouns (*D.*, pp. 562–3), those, Abelard says, regarding not the 'nominatio' (otherwise all general nouns would be so) but only their 'significatio'. These observations appear in *G.G.*, pp. 117–22, that is, at the beginning of the comment on the *Categorie* of *Ingredientibus*; one can also see a basic agreement in both texts. See also *D.*, pp. 181 (25–37) and 222 (29–31); pp. 592ff.

36 *G.G.*, pp. 21 (26) and 22 (6).

37 *G.G.*, pp. 22 (2–4), 26 (29–32), 30 (1–5), 525 (2), 115 (30), 116 (17), 112–3.

38 *G.G.*, pp. 45–7.

39 See *G.G.*, p. 546 (3–9 and 36–8).

40 *D.*, p. 112 (24): "Alii enim omnia quibus vox imposita est ab ipsa voce significari volunt...."

41 *G.G.*, pp. 326 (16) and 327 (14).

42 From *G.G.*, pp. 325–9 Abelard in fact examines the various types of 'intellectus', or rather the different ways of comprehension determined by one or

more 'voces': 'intellectus simplex', 'compositus', 'unus', 'sanus' and 'verus'.
43 *D.*, p. 153 (9); "Scientia est comprehensio veritas."
44 *G.G.*, p. 326 (30–1).
45 The 'res' is always 'discreta': see *G.G.*, p. 30 (6–8).
46 *G.G.*, p. 19 (21–5).
47 *G.G.*, p. 136 (22–4).
48 See for example the passage *G.L.*, p. 31 (19–30), where the validity of the
sermon based on reality is affirmed. Other passages: *G.G.*, p. 532 (3–8), 36 (47),
537 (7–10), 136 (7–10).
49 *G.G.*, p. 23.
50 *G.G.*, p. 337ff.; *D.*, p. 118ff. The Abelardian position on this problem is
complex and made articulate in the two solutions in *Ingredientibus* and *Dialectica*. (In the literal notes of the Palatine Master, which adhere fundamentally to
the Aristotelian text which does not examine the 'dictiones indefinitae', he does
not allude to the problem of their meaning.) In the comment, Abelard excludes
prepositions and conjunctions from the definition of 'voces significativae per
se' and shows their semantic value in the 'consignificatio' or in the signification
of an 'actio' (and not of a concept). A cross-reference to Priscian shows how the
grammatical view justifies a study of these 'voces' more than the strictly logical
ambit (*G.G.*, pp. 339–40). The position in the second text is different: firstly it is
in *Dialectica* that Abelard calls them 'dictiones indefinitae', which, compared
to the definition of 'dictio (*D.*, p. 118 (9–10)) implies a 'significatio per se',
namely complete even if indeterminate, while this was excluded in the comment
(*G.G.*, p. 337). Also of interest is the cross-reference made by Abelard to the
'dialectici' quoted by Boetius whose inquiry on these parts of the discourse
understood as 'colligamenta' rests on the affirmations of the same. These
dialecticians might be the ones mentioned by Priscian (see Preti, 'La vox significativa nella semantica terministica', *Rivista critica di storia della filosofia* **10**
(1955) p. 260), given the coincidence of the opinions. In any case, the position
of *Dialectica* in this respect is all the more novel and interesting as it promotes
a positive consideration and an inquiry into these 'voces' in the Stoic rather
than in the Aristotelian line, which was then taken up by the terministic logicians
of the 13th century. The passage in *Dialectica* is certainly more critical and
mature than the corresponding passage from the comment, and it constitutes
the first treatment of the 'syncathegoremata' in the history of mediaeval logic
(see Preti, *op.cit.*, p. 261, who had settled the beginning of the treatment of the
'voces consignificativae' as being in William of Shyreswood's treatise; the
article appeared in 1955, however, that is, before the complete edition of
Dialectica).
51 It will be as well to examine Abelard's considerations of the verb. To a large
extent they are an illustration of the Aristotelian definition (Aristotle, *De
Interpretatione*, Minio edition, 1.6b 5–25; *G.L.*, pp. 79–80; *G.G.*, pp. 34–5;
D., p. 129).

Abelard insistently specifies that the distinction between noun and verb can
only be made if based on the copulative function of the verb and its 'consignificatio temporis', as opposed to any other possible discriminatory criterion
(*G.G.*, pp. 346 (25–6), 348, 353; *D.*, pp. 129–30).

He gives full and original consideration to his inquiry into the 'vis predicationis' of the verb and the various types of 'copulatio' in the comment of *Ingredientibus* and in the treatment of *Dialectica*; and, inasfar as the comment of the Literal Notes is not detached from the content of the Aristotelian treatments, Abelard's particular interest in this argument, in this text as well, is testified to by a certain breadth of the notes (*G.L.*, pp. 79–84). The careful Abelardian observations on the functions of the verb do not derive from the parallel Aristotelian passage, but – if one considers the frequent cross-references Abelard makes to Priscian – (*G.G.*, pp. 346, 348, 359, 360; *D.*, p. 132) seem to refer rather to an Aristotelian-Boetian type of consideration, which is closer to the nature of Stoic than Aristotelian inquiry.

Abelard singles out two functions of the verb: the predicative of something, and the copulative (*G.G.*, p. 359; *D.*, pp. 131–2). The first is based on the potentiality of the verb as a 'vox significativa'; the second is the feature that distinguishes the verb from the noun (*G.G.*, pp. 348, 353).

Most verbs, because of the type of meaning they have, can only copulate themselves (*G.G.*, p. 359; *D.*, pp. 132–3); only appellative verbs and the 'substantivum' can copulate other than with themselves (*G.G.*, p. 359). While the first can only copulate nouns – because of their 'significatio' which in the specific sense is the 'nuncupatio' (*G.G.*, p. 363; *D.*, p. 134), the second "quod seque omnia secundum essentiam significat, quaslibet essentias potest copulare". (*D.*, p. 131 (23–6); *G.G.*, p. 360)).

From this one can see how the type of copulative function of a verb depends on the nature of its 'significatio'.

52 See *D.*, p. 121 (1–26).
53 *G.G.*, p. 140 (13–24).
54 See *G.G.*, pp. 21 (36–8), 22 (1–2).

CHAPTER III

THE MEANING OF UNIVERSAL NOUNS

I

As has already been remarked, an examination of the Abelardian doctrine of universals is of particular interest in the discussion of the 'significatio' of a noun.

I also think that an inquiry of this sort has its *raison d'être* (this is the most widely known part of the Palatine Master's logical works) if it tries to clarify the reason for the opposite verdict, of which the doctrine itself has been made a sign.

Another reason is the noticeable if not radical change of attitude in Abelard in the treatment of the problem, from the note in *Ingredientibus* to the note in *Nostrorum*.

It will thus be helpful to follow the exposition of the doctrine separately in the various texts.

In the *Glosse Letterali* – commenting on the *Isagoge* with a note supporting the Porphyrian text – Abelard, together with the author, refuses to reply to the 'altissimum negotium', or rather refuses to resolve the 'quaestiones' that Porphyrius poses.[1]

As we do not have any definite position, our study will consist of selecting from the comment some of Abelard's typical expressions which we shall use as indications of his attitude.

First and foremost it must be emphasised that for Abelard Porphyrius' intention was definitely an examination of the 'voces', "quoniam ex istis sex vocibus constituuntur praedicamenta".[2]

This interpretation does not come to him from the Boetian translation in which the ambiguity of the Porphyrian text was so loose, but in the opposite direction, in affirming namely that the matter in question was a speculation on things.[3]

Not only does the investigation into the genus and species have a direction 'vocalis' for Abelard, but – to indicate how aware this attitude is – he embodies this treatment, as belonging to the 'scientia inveniendi', in the schema of logic: "quia hic docemur invenire rationes sufficientes ad probandas quaestiones factas de istis sex vocibus et de significatis earum."[4]

The nominalistic attitude is evident, even if there is no declared choice of the attribution of the definition of universals to 'voces', if we situate the problems concerning the types in the semantic problem and omit metaphysical complications within the limitations of this inquiry.[5]

A whole hierarchy of nouns is thus created, starting from the individual which "praedicatur de uno solo"[6] and ending with the ten 'generalissima', also 'voces', which are no longer comprehensible under the 'nomen' 'ens' because of the ambiguity.[7]

There is another significant passage in the treatise *De indifferentia*, where Abelard distinguishes the real plane (which justifies and permits the predication) and the plane of the 'voces': "... si homo constituitur ex animali materialiter et ex rationali formaliter, tunc animal praedicatur de homine in quid et rationale in quale."[8]

Taking into account this and the previously emphasised statements[9], we can conclude that this is in substance the typical attitude that Abelard entertains in his whole logical inquiry: on the one hand he refuses absolutely to develop, as a dialectician, an investigation that does not focus exclusively on the 'voces' established in the signification, thus excluding the study of 'res' from the sphere of logic, and their relations; on the other he more or less explicitly bases the relations of predication and the rules of discourse on the relations of things.

Another point worth noting appears to be the acritical qualification of universals as 'voces' and the refusal of the inherent problematic: this probably indicates an influence of Roscellin's solution and thus implicitly implies the critique of realism that Abelard's first master must have developed in his instruction and which constituted the psychological motivation of the Abelardian procedure in this comment.[10]

II

The first explicit formulation[11] known to us of the Abelardian theory of universals is in *Ingredientibus*.

Here Abelard openly broaches the polemic and, before establishing his 'sententia', he expounds and criticises the doctrines which had been forming, with his personal and habitual method.

The point of departure is the Aristotelian definition, while the alternative of the positions possible is that with Boetian origins[12]: 'res seu voces'.[13] We shall have to see to which of these two terms the definition is adjusted ("de pluribus quod natum est aptum praedicari") – the definition put forward as a criterion.

The polemic in which Abelard intervenes is a current one: in fact the trustees of the 'auctoritas' could both second the theses.

Abelard thus proceeds to examine the statement of the first position of his contemporaries.[14]

The 'sententia', which attributes the definition of universals to realities, takes up two positions.

The first could be called integral realism: it affirms the unity of the essence that "eodem tempore idem totum in diversis" is the basis of the existence of the individuals that are only distinct "per advenientes formas".[15]

Singling out the 'quidam' supporters of the theory is helped by evidence of Guillaume de Champeaux's thought contained in a letter from Abelard himself.[16]

Referring to the first formulation of Guillaume's doctrine of universals, Abelard reports two typical and basic expressions of the doctrine which is examined and commented upon in our text: (a) "...eamdem essentialiter rem totam simul singulis suis inesse"; (b) "...nulla...in essentia diversitas, sed sola multitudine accidentium varietas".

These expressions appear significant because both in them and in the critical exposition of *Ingredientibus* one can detect on the one hand the affirmation of the unity of 'subsistentia' of the universal and its basic and unique character which is contemporary with all individual existences, and on the other the affirmation of the fundamentality of the varieties of accidental forms to distinguish the individuals.

The Abelardian criticism uses metaphysical and logical arguments: there is no reference to theological principles, to which he resorts, however, in *Nostrorum*.

The very complete[17] argumentation is based on the inevitable (at times the absolute identity of the essence is laid down) simultaneity of the opposites[18], physically inconceivable and opposed to the invoked principle of non-contradiction.[19]

The development of the argumentation, going from type to type, shows that, owing to a unique essence and the variety of the forms which result as impossible, the whole world should be reduced to the immutability of the ten 'generalissima'.[20]

The second realistic position, which is shrewder, is the 'indifferentia' of the substance, and the separation 'essentialiter' of individual things is affirmed.[21]

This is worked out in two formulations: the doctrine of the 'collectio' and the doctrine of the 'convenientia'.

The supporters of the former say that the 'res universalis' has a collective character which thus consists in a grouping of singles[22]; for those who support the latter, the universal is simply the individual considered in its 'convenientia', by virtue of a 'similitudo naturae'.[23]

Abelard's letter, quoted earlier, mentions a theory of 'indifferentia' and attributes it to Guillaume, who, in this position, probably took refuge because of the effective criticism of his disciple.[24]

The Master would therefore have maintained that the universal is not a unique common essence, but that it results simply from the lack of differentiation of the individuals, or rather their similarity: "... rem eamdem non essentialiter sed indifferenter ...."

One can note two points from this very brief exposition of Guillaume's theory: firstly the affirmation that the universal belongs to the order of reality, as in the first formula of solution; secondly, the substitution of the concept of similarity for that of identity.[25]

One can, more specifically, observe that in Abelard's times

Gauslenus de Soissons[26] spoke of the 'collectio' as a 'res universalis' but the vague information we have about him and the brevity of Abelard's exposition mean that it is only a hypothesis that Abelard meant to refer to the doctrine stated by him when he talks of 'collectio'; and the most diligent informer, John of Salisbury, makes no mention of the 'convenientia' theory which shows a certain terminological assonance with the 'causa communis' doctrine which Abelard expounds in *Ingredientibus*.

One can see how this is the formulation, in positive terms and specific terms, of the 'indifferentia' theory of substance; that is, it affirms that the universal is that natural 'similitudo' that makes a group of individuals undifferentiated.[27]

Criticism of these positions is subtle and the refusal of realism is complete. With regard to the supporters of the first, Abelard objects that a genus understood as a 'collectio' does not have the possibility of being totally the predicate of an individual; in addition he points out that infinite species are created with arbitrary regroupings.[28]

As for the 'convenientia' theory, Abelard first of all observes that the identification of 'praedicari de pluribus' with 'convenire cum pluribus' is absurd; this would, by analogy, result with the individual who is predicated by one alone having to "convenire cum una tantum re"; furthermore there would no longer be any criterion of discrimination between the individual and the universal. This indiscrimination would in fact result from two statements from which Abelard borrows the contradictoriness: on the one side the universal belongs to the order of reality, on the other it consists in an aspect that belongs to the individual (that 'natura consimilis' which allows the 'convenientia' of several individuals). Consequently 'homo' is no more than 'Socrates' and the latter is at once the universal 'res' and the individual.

I would say that Abelard's last criticism is fundamental: where, he asks, do the different individuals agree? And he excludes any treatment of a "convenientia in re speciali", given that the existence of these 'res' has already been shown to be impossible.[29]

The Palatine Master's comment on this doctrine stresses clearly its weakness which derives from the hybrid nature of the basic conception; in fact he wants to maintain the statement that the universal is a 'res' and at the same time he concedes that the only existing thing is the individual, which is why the species becomes an aspect of this.

This realistic doctrine is therefore without the Platonic character which was part of the first doctrine examined by Abelard.

The result of Abelard's critical examination can be summed up in the decisive repudiation of the statement that universals are realities, no matter how these realities can be conceived.

For his part, Abelard had already stated that the problem of universals was a problem of predication[30] and this statement clarifies the position that he assumes in the polemic.

The 'vis praedicationis' is distinct from the purely constructive one of grammarians by requiring a true or false signification; Abelard here takes the Aristotelian line and says he takes reality as a controlling criterion.

Having posed the alternative whether the Aristotelian definition could be adapted to things or words, Abelard arrived by exclusion at the statement that universals are 'voces'. If he uses the term 'vox' in the formula of solution to indicate universals, one must take into account that the species is straight away afterwards called 'nomen', 'vocabulum', and 'sermo'.[31]

This narrows the terminological difference between the solution of *Ingredientibus* and that of *Nostrorum*, and shows that the term 'sermo' was used at least normally, if not frequently. In this way the value of 'vox' is also specified, which, excluding special aspects, is the simple physical sound.

The inquiry into the meaning of these 'voces' thus constitutes the most prominent section of the Abelardian doctrine.

The semantic value of a noun consists either in a direct and complete relation: 'vox'-'res', or in a potentiality of the 'vox' to produce an 'intellectus' ("significare est constituere intellectum"[32], which in order to be valid must still rely on a structure that corresponds to the real.[33]

The signification of single words is valid because of the first type of reason, given that these words reflect the world of 'res' which exist 'discrete'.[34]

But because Abelard destroys, critically, the Platonic universal 'res', the doubt remains whether the 'intellectus' to which the common 'voces' refer is null. [35]

At this point we can already see the outline of the direction in which he will develop his investigation: first, a natural ordering that justifies the imposition of these 'voces' must be found, and thereby one will see the foundation of the 'intellectus' that results from it.

He therefore in the first instance turns to the study of the 'causa communis impositionis' which he selects by the 'status' which individual things – though quite distinct – possess: Socrates and Plato are similar in their human status.[36]

With regard to this solution it should be noted that Abelard insists on making it distinct from the realistic position that affirmed the substantiality of that which makes the individuals identical. Despite the refusal of the concept of identity, which in the first doctrine commented on implied the substantiality of the common element[37], we find in the Abelardian solution the explicit and insistent statement of the 'non-res' nature of the 'status': this, Abelard maintains, is not essence, but only a way of being.[38]

The 'causa communis' theory shows undeniable analogies of terminology with the exposition of the 'convenientia' doctrine of *Ingredientibus* and of *Nostrorum*.[39]

Despite this, it seems to me that the doctrine criticised and the exposition of the 'causa communis' doctrine[40] should not be as-similated for two basic reasons:

(a) the 'convenientia' doctrine is a statement of the reality of universals, while the Abelardian doctrine is set up as a basis of meaning of universal nouns, whose vocal nature has already been insisted upon. The two views are thus polemically opposed;

(b) Abelard insists strongly on the refusal of any substantialistic interpretation of the 'status'.[41] This makes the Abelardian position conscious of the danger into which the 'causa communis' doctrine runs and stresses the distinction between the two theories.

However, the undeniable similarity that is already visible in *Ingredientibus* between the formula of a commented doctrine and the author's proposed solution puts the latter in a particular situation which develops, in *Nostrorum*, on the one hand into the absence of the 'causa communis' theory, on the other into the clear refusal of the 'convenientia statu' doctrine.

Having exhausted the investigation of the 'causa communis' we can now examine the elements in which the 'intellectus' of universal nouns consist.[42]

If we refer back to some of the observations in Chapter II[43] and keep in mind the 'nominatio-significatio' distinction which is also confirmed in this section of *Ingredientibus*[44], we can at once conclude that the field of the 'nominatio' carries no weight for Abelard in this inquiry; the world of universal 'res' has been critically destroyed. The 'conceptio' solicited by the general noun will appear on the primary plane and will qualify the universal noun as such.

Abelard characterises this 'conceptio' as "communis et confusa", while the form of the singular 'intellectus' is precise and concerns one single determined object.[45]

The 'conceptio' solicited by the 'vox' universal concerns several things (interconnected by a common 'status'), but does not belong to any of them if taken individually: 'homo' means only the general concept, although it speaks of individuals.[46]

This causes the indeterminateness of the 'intellectus' of universal nouns, which, as happens for the individual 'voces', do not exactly reproduce reality and yet, by reflecting a feature of it, present themselves as legitimate.[47]

If, when referring to a passage from Priscian – already used elsewhere[48] – and comparing the general 'intellectus' (in the sense of form) to the divine ideas 'ante creationem', the author says our 'opiniones' are rather this than 'intellectus', he then immediately affirms the validity and nature of acts of intelligence because of the real structure which confirms them as 'causa communis': the 'status'.[49]

The inquiry into the objective legitimising criterion and its elements of the 'conceptio' of universal nouns led Abelard to examine the intellectual process which, from the consideration of reality, led to the 'formae'.

The process, Abelard then says, is one of abstraction: the intellect takes the different aspects of one thing into consideration, or rather it considers 'separatim' matter and form, which, 'separata', are not in reality.[50]

This produces the statement that the 'modus intelligendi' is different from the 'modus subsistendi' for the reason that, in the production of universal 'intellectus' the thing is conceived 'aliter quam sit' even if it is not 'alia quam sit'.[51]

The Abelardian theory of abstraction, compared with the Aristotelian theory, presents a very significant originality[52]; this, together with the replacement of the 'status' by the universal 'res' and the statement that the value of the 'modus intelligendi' does not consist in a mere reproduction of the real, achieves a distinction, within determined limits[53], of the objective meaning of a class of nouns from the plane of the 'res'.[54]

In order to integrate the Abelardian doctrine of universals in *Ingredientibus*, it is interesting to refer back to some of Abelard's notes in the comment on *De Interpretatione*. As well as the reaffirmed element of 'non-res' of the 'formae imaginariae'[55], the object both of the intellective 'actio' and the imagination, there are two types of consideration which are of particular interest:

(a) Abelard says: nouns have a 'significatio perfecta', "quaecumque in nominibus versantur ea neque sensus neque imaginationes, sed solam significare intellectus qualitatem"[56];

(b) He affirms that in the intellective act the property and the nature of things are considered.[57]

Linking this last point to the statement that the meanings of universals are based on a 'causa' constituted by a determined 'natura' of 'res'[58], we can with safety conclude that the meaning of universals has nothing to do with the 'imaginatio'[59]; this is even confirmed by point (a).

By affirming that the form, towards which the intellect, urged by the universal noun, is directed, is vague ('vaga')[60], Abelard does not then want to allude to its lesser dignity by placing it closer to opinion, as a type of knowledge, than to intelligence[61], but he is simply pointing to the lesser determinateness that the 'conceptio' of universals has, due to the spreading of the significative sphere from the nominative to the intellective plane, but still maintaining this 'similitudo'.

In replying to the Porphyrian 'quaestiones', Abelard deliberately takes the terms in a non-literal meaning, which does not therefore adhere to the realistic mentality which presides over the formulation of the same. And this so as to be able to use the questions themselves. All the points of the doctrine examined are completely confirmed in Abelard's replies.[62]

A fourth question is formulated by Abelard alone, and just as those of Porphyrius are symptomatic of a realistic-Platonic mentality, so this is indicative of the anti-realistic position that the author has assumed from the outset. Abelard asks himself, "Nominatis rebus destructis", what happens to the meaning of the universal 'voces'! And he replies that the signification persists in the negative propositions ("nulla rosa est").[63] If we keep in mind the separation of the 'significatio' from the 'nominatio' the reason is clear: the meaning is given by the intellective sphere, not by the real sphere, and therefore when things no longer exist (which is not the same as 'they have never existed')[64] the 'intellectus' will still provide a meaning for 'vox', although this does not claim to refer to existing things and nominated things (that is, the 'significatio' will only subsist in negative propositions).

Alongside the theory of the 'status', this statement of the permanence of the signification independently of the permanence of the thing nominated is a sign of the process of distinction between the world of the 'nomina' and an immediate relation with the world of the real.

III

The exposition of the various 'sententiae' in *Nostrorum* is more complex. Here too the point of reference is the Aristotelian definition which is joined – always stressing the element of predicability – by the expression "quod de subiecto dicitur".[65]

The schema though is the same: to see what this definition is adapted to. But there are three solutions: 'ad res', 'ad intellectus', 'ad sermones'.[66] The different attitude results, apparently at least, from the fusion of the two alternatives: the Boetian ('res-vox') and the Porphyrian ('res-intellectus').

There is an immediate and decisive statement: Abelard notes that from the Aristotelian definition it follows inevitably that universals are 'sermones' because it is only proper for 'sermones' to be preached; universality is a property of some of these.[67]

But let us now examine the 'sententiae'.

The first is divided into various 'opiniones'.[68]

The exposition of the realistic and most radical theory is in every way similar to that of *Ingredientibus* and embodies the 'brunellus' argument which, in this, was more precisely part of the criticism. The contradictions in which it is involved are those that have already been noted in the previous text complicated by the theological consequences.[69] In fact, by the reduction of all substances to the single 'generalissima' substance, the divine substance would also be identical to others: 'pessima haeresis'.

It is true, Abelard observes, that, confirmed by authority, there is the thesis that God cannot really be called substance, a thesis which was favourably received by dialecticians – as Abelard mentions –, who were thus liberated from theological preoccupations.[70] Abelard leaves the problem open, limiting himself to expounding the contrasting evidence with a method similar to the *Sic et non* method[71], and to indicating the solution in the two possible exceptions to the term 'substantia', the 'largior' and the 'strictior': the theological problem is reintroduced into a semantic problem.

In the exposition of the 'indifferentia' theory one can detect a slight change with regard to *Ingredientibus*; the nature of the universal whereby this consists in the different 'respectus' with which the particular is considered (only the existing particular) is accentuated.[72]

The exposition refers to that of the same doctrine in *De generibus et speciebus*.[73] In the passage in this text which concerns the illustration of the 'sententia de indifferentia' we can in fact note: (a) the statement that the only existence is the individual existence ("...nihil est praeter individuum"); (b) that the universal is simply the individual 'aliter attentus'; (c) and that the individual is universal inasmuch as it has a universal 'natura' or 'status'.

All three points are present in the inquiry Abelard makes into the doctrine 'de indifferentia', the third being particularly notable as it affirms: "...Aliquis status est participatione cuius multae sunt convenientes."[74] There are two reasons why this last statement is of particular interest: on the one hand there was no hint of an 'indifferentia statu' in the exposition of the 'de indifferentia' doctrine of *Ingredientibus*, but only of an 'indifferentia natura'[75]; on the other, we have seen Abelard in *Ingredientibus*, propose the meaning of universal nouns as the real and legitimising foundation – a real doctrine of the 'status communis'.[76]

In the criticism of the 'indifferentia' theory of *Nostrorum* one might therefore see a self-criticism of the position of *Ingredientibus*, and this could be confirmed by the fact that in *Nostrorum* Abelard no longer proposes the doctrine of the 'status communis' as the 'causa impositionis'. Consideration of the following points nevertheless seems to oppose this interpretation:

(a) The statement of the 'indifferentia statu' assimilated to the 'indifferentia natura' was already present in the formulation of the 'de indifferentia' theory, as is shown by the passage from *De generibus et speciebus*;

(b) In *Ingredientibus* Abelard had not said that the universal was that on which the individuals agree (or rather the 'natura' or the 'status'), but that the universal 'vox' based its own meaning on this real status;

(c) if it is true that the 'status' theory is no longer explicitly present in *Nostrorum*, the legitimising foundation of universal nouns is indicated, in this text as well, in an element with which the individual 'res' are endowed.

It seems to me, therefore, that the change in terminology observed in the examination of the 'indifferentia' theory, between *Ingredientibus* and *Nostrorum*, is more an indication of a severe

and radical position being taken up by Abelard in the face of a
realistic doctrine than a refusal of a personal doctrine and a consequent change.[77]

It is certain that Abelard, by underlining the statement of the
'indifferentia statu', pushed his anti-realistic polemic to the limit
and shows that he feels the need for attenuating the consideration
and real foundation of universal nouns; this is confirmed by the
absence, in *Nostrorum*, of the 'causa communis' theory.

The criticism of the 'indifferentia' doctrine is developed parallel
with that of the preceding text, even if at greater length.[78]

Abelard then passes to an examination of a theory that is not
explicitly coincidental with the 'collectio' theory, but which can be
assimilated to it; in fact it points at the plurality, composed of
single individuals, the characteristic of the universal, affirming that
it is a property that single things can have by uniting together,
while, forced away from the 'collectio', they are individual.[79] But
this theory lacks the criterion of a rigorous differentiation between
individual and universal, and Abelard rebukes this indiscrimination,
observing that it is not enough for a community to create the
species that would thus consist in an arbitrary regrouping of
individuals and would not have any exclusive properties.[80]

The lack of an identity of terminology prevents us from recog-
nising even the minimal amount we know about Gauslenus de
Soissons' theory in this exposition.[81]

Following the schema that Abelard advanced, we should at this
point find an investigation of the 'intellectus' theory. But in fact
what follows is the exposition of the 'sermones' doctrine, which is
polemically distinct from the 'voces' doctrine".[82]

In this respect one can observe that a theory that affirmed the
species solely as 'intellectus' was never outlined as an autonomous
guide in the polemic of the universals[83]: this seems confirmed as
well by certain passages taken by Prantl which are evidence that
the dilemma was posed by the 'sententia vocum' and 'sententia
rerum'[84], and also by the allusion of John of Salisbury to those
who affirmed that the universals are 'intellectus'.[85]

In fact this passage, which is incidentally very short, contains no indication to the supporters of this doctrine and traces it back to Cicero and Boetius. In these two and in Aristotle the 'intellectus' acts as intermediary rather than constituting a third term. It is precisely this type of 'intellectus', understood as 'excogitatio', that Abelard mentions, but at the same time (and this indiscrimination indicates a certain confusion of concepts) he alludes to the "intellectus in divina mente".[86] For the second there is a reference to the 'auctoritas' of Priscian and Plato: this type of 'intellectus' remains absolutely alien to the problem of universals, as presented in a comment on the *Isagoge*, given that the term of the discussion is not given by the archetypal ideas in God but by the types and species of natural beings.[87]

The other type of 'intellectus', on the other hand, is relinked to the considerations of the intellective act of abstraction, present in Boetius, which are taken up again by Abelard and set up by him as the basis of the meaning of universal nouns.

Abelard therefore stops, as in the preceding text, at the criticism of the realistic doctrine; the polemic he conducts against the universal understood as 'vox' is more like a specification in the sphere of the 'sermo' doctrine than a criticism of an autonomous position.

In the formula of the Abelardian solution one should note: the wary tone with which Abelard first puts forward his doctrine ("Est alia universalibus sententia rationi vicinior...")[88] and the immediately following polemic against the 'vox' theory. The attitude of being predicated – a basic feature of the universal –, which is clearly stressed by the Aristotelian formula, is proper only to the 'sermo' because of the human 'institutio'.[89]

By attributing to the 'vox' – a pure physical sound – Aristotle's definition, one would be saying that a 'res' is in several 'res', which has already been shown to be impossible.[90]

One can therefore quickly see the meaning – different to that of *Ingredientibus* – in which Abelard uses the term 'vox' in this text. From the considerations of *Ingredientibus* it emerged quite plainly that with 'vox' the element indicated was the word set up for the signification; in *Nostrorum* Abelard uses 'vox' to mean what he had called 'materia nominis' in *Ingredientibus*.[91]

Both in *Ingredientibus* and in *Nostrorum*[92] Abelard uses the term 'nomen' (in the Aristotelian-Boetian meaning), which he assimilates in the first text to 'vox' and in the second to 'sermo', thus making it distinct from 'vox'. The use of the term in both texts confirms the substantial identity of the formulae of solution which Abelard proposes to the 'quaestio' on universals: by universal Abelard means, in both comments, the vocal symbol that the 'impositio hominum' has charged with the designatory function of a certain 'intellectus'.

A passage from *Ingredientibus* confirms this still further: "Vox communi, cum quasi una res essentia in se sit...secundum... appellationem, non secundum essentiam suam de pluribus est praedicabilis...."[93] It is clear not only that Abelard meant to designate, with the term 'vox', the word established in the signification, but also that he had already seen the need that leads him to the distinction of *Nostrorum*, not turned against the previous text, but a development of it. The only differences therefore consist in the variation that the use of 'vox' undergoes[94] and in the urgent need, felt in the second text, to insist on the institutive operation.

This could also be due to the desire to avoid the insinuating interpretation, evident in the words of Anselm, which the previous formula could fall into[95], as well, of course, as the interest which Abelard would have had in distinguishing his own position from that of Roscellin.[96]

Abelard skilfully achieves this end, upsetting the value of the statement "universale est vox": he accuses this formula of realism because in it the universal is attributed with the natural character of physical reality and that artificial character of 'nota' is not stressed: the genus – Abelard frequently repeats – is the articulate sound selected by men for 'generare intellectum', i.e., it is the 'sermo'.[97]

The insistence on the artificiality as a basic feature of the human discourse is the most typical trait of Abelard's attitude in *Nostrorum*.

Apart from the historical reasons that may have led to a more rigorous terminological specification, the 'sermo' doctrine and the criticism of the 'vox' doctrine[98] of *Nostrorum* fit exactly into the general frame of this work and coincide with another reason: the wider and more complete criticism of the realistic theory and the absence of a 'causa communis' doctrine.[99]

The study of the value of universal nouns in *Nostrorum* is thus more complex than it was in *Ingredientibus*, where Abelard had put forward the 'status communis' theory, immediately after the statement that the only realities are the individuals.[100]

First of all he denies that single things are meant by the universal noun[101]: the 'nominatio-significatio' distinction, having operated in an anti-Platonic direction, assumes an implicit critical bearing, also when confronted with the Aristotelian position.

One can only refer back to Abelard's replies to the Porphyrian 'quaestiones': these agree in every way with those of *Ingredientibus*, but have a greater importance because of the lack both of a 'causa impositionis' theory and of a study of the value of the 'intellectus' comparable to those of the previous text.

The first 'quaestio' is understood as in *Ingredientibus*: if the types and species subsist or are "in opinione cassa sine re".[102] Abelard's reply is that the types, like expressions, 'appellant' (they do not signify) existing or rather single things[103]; as for the other alternative, they are put in intellects that are free from any sensorial fetter[104], that is, one should understand that their reference to single things is by nature certainly not fettered by the quality of presence of the things themselves. The 'nudus' of the Porphyrian 'quaestio' is understood by Abelard as an allusion to the independence of these 'intellectus' from accidental and individual forms[105], while 'purus', which exists neither in the Porphyrian text[106] nor in the Boetian translation[107], is seen to indicate the fact that single things are not contained as such in universal nouns, but are admitted to participate in a community.[108]

The second question, likewise – Abelard observes – can only be used in a figurative sense, literally indicating a subsistence of the types which has already been denied; the author also observes that he will take 'corporeo' as distinct (in fact the corporeality with the determination of the space occupied suggests the distinction) and 'incorporeo' as indistinct.[109] The reply is thus this: universals nominate distinct things in an indistinct manner.[110] This implicitly confirms the 'confusus' nature of the intellects of universals.

The reply to the third 'quaestio' is interesting because the distinction of the two planes, significative and appellative, on which the explanation of the Abelardian position of *Ingredientibus* is based, is clearly confirmed.

Abelard's reply is in fact: "...Genera et species in sensibilibus posita sunt per appelationem, extra vero per significationem."[111]

Unfortunately the reply to the question, which as early as in *Ingredientibus* Abelard had linked to the Porphyrian ones, is incomprehensible in this text; in fact the example of the chimera, "cum nulla rem continet", is certainly not suited to the investigation if, when things are destroyed, the significance of the universal in negative propositions still remains.[112]

The first and second Abelardian replies therefore seem worth noting as the Palatine Master reproposes, in a minimised way, something very similar to the objective cause of the value of universals and moreover points to the indeterminateness of the 'conceptio' of general nouns.

Having reported an already quoted Boetian argumentation against the subsistence of universals[113], Abelard says the remaining part, aimed at showing the vanity of the universal 'intellectus' inasfar as they are deprived of the 'res' lying below, is sophistry.[114] Unlike *Ingredientibus*, we do not, however, have any recall to an already developed doctrine on their legitimate formation, but only a generic affirmation that the 'intelligere' in its 'modus' is not strictly bound to the 'modus subsistendi', and it is possible, and not in vain, to conceive the thing 'aliter quam sit' namely to take one single aspect of a thing whereas 'in re' this is always in combination with others.[115]

Abelard therefore announces an examination of various points: "De significatione et intellectu eorum; quam doctrinam faciant quamque commoda sit impositio eorum."[116]

The second and third points are present for the first time in *Nostrorum*; the first is concerned with seeing the value of the concept solicited by universal nouns. It is clear – Abelard confirms – that this does not consist in a reference to single things; on the contrary, it is concerned, in the name of man, with 'intelligere' human nature in general, namely 'animal rationale mortale'.

The meaning is therefore given by a mental object independent of the 'res' or, better, not explicitly bound to them by that chain which was the 'status' in the previous text. Abelard calls this mental object 'conceptio simplex'; in it – he observes – man is considered indifferently "absque ulla certitudine personae"[117] and if he asks himself what the validity of it is he replies with a psychological-pragmatic motivation: "... secundum eorum intellectum multa sane possunt deliberari".[118]

The doctrine of the universal 'sermones' – Abelard goes on – orders the assignation of nouns suited to indicate that things, though absolutely distinct, show aspects due to which it is possible to consider them in a community.[119]

This is to say that the fact that there is a certain 'convenientia' between the 'discrete' things is affirmed. Consequently an objective type of motivation is still present as the basis of the meaning of universals, although the 'causa communis' doctrine is missing.

The practical character of the 'impositio' cause of universals is reconsidered in the examination of whether their imposition is useful; Abelard here replies by saying that through the infinity and inconstancy of existing individuals one resorts more exactly and more conveniently to universal nouns if one wants to extend the predication to all individuals.[120]

But the section *De generibus* closes with a more decisive and interesting statement.[121] It aims at validifying the intellect of universals by enlarging the legitimate sphere of meaning. (There is no need – Abelard says – for there to be a 'res' constantly beneath the intellective act in order to make it sound, just as the existence of the thing desired is not necessary when an act of will is formulated.) And up to this point we are dealing with that type of consideration which had led him to say that the abstractive process in the production of universal forms was legitimate, in *Ingredientibus*; but immediately after this Abelard stresses the autonomous character of the 'intelligere' to the point of not distinguishing it any longer from what he had elsewhere called 'opinio'.[122]

"Cum igitur chimeram intellego, etsi nulla res est, aliquid tamen intellego." Here is the antipodes of St. Anselm's 'intelligere', which implied and exhausted the reality of what was thought and also of the 'intelligere' to which Abelard alludes elsewhere.

The Abelardian solution of *Nostrorum*, apart from a greater preoccupation with terminological accuracy, does not seem to present an effective deepening of the 'quaestio': the metaphysical view still bears substantially on semantic inquiry, and in addition psychological-pragmatic elements are present. In my opinion the position of *Nostrorum* is hallmarked by a certain instability[123]; on the one hand the points which guaranteed the doctrine of the previous text are put in the shade, even if maintained; on the other one cannot find any new positive path of study.

Even the most intransigent anti-realistic attitude, which leads Abelard (a) to accentuate his criticism of realistic positions and (b) to eliminate the 'causa communis' doctrine, is not resolved in a real contribution to the inquiry into the value of general nouns, because it does not manage to inspire a new attitude to the problem.

This would add further interest to an acquaintance with other Abelardian formulations of the theory of universals.

IV

As is well-known, *Dialectica* has come down to us without the part dedicated to the treatment of universals. De Rijk has reconstructed the structure of the 'volumen' I helped by Abelard's reference in the first book *De substantia* of 'volumen' II (*Praedicamenta*): "...Sicut Secundus Antepraedicamentorum de differentia continet." From this it has been deduced that the 'volumen' *Antepraedicamenta* dealt with universals or Porphyrian 'quinque voces'; that the second book of this 'volumen' was dedicated to the *Differentia* and that therefore, as volumes II and III of the first treatise each consist of three books, it is very likely that 'volumen' I was composed likewise.

De Rijk places the treatment of the genus and the species to book I, the treatment of the 'differentia' to book II, and the treatment of the proper and the accident to book III.[124]

There is absolutely no explicit statement of any position being taken up by the author with regard to the problem of universals. This would most probably have been at the beginning of book I.

In the context of *Dialectica* as a whole there are, however, references to universals, to the problem of their meaning and also to the 'quaestio' regarding them. As well as this, our understanding of the Abelardian position in this text is helped by the very general considerations of the 'significatio' of a noun, which have been examined in the preceding chapter.[125]

This fragmentary material must, however, be used with caution because the passages concerning universals do not belong to a systematic exposition, and Abelard can therefore allow himself to use expressions which are not as precise as one would need if one were dealing with the explicit formulation of his doctrine.[126]

First of all one can ask: are universals nouns in *Dialectica* as well?

A passage belonging to *De definitis* indicates the Abelardian position on this point: "Sunt autem quaedam nominum proprietates iuxta significationem pensandae, quaedam vero secundum positionem constructionis attendendae, quaedam etiam secundum vocis compositionem accipiendae."[127]

Among the properties of the first type we find why a noun is universal. The following extract also tells what 'genus' and 'species' nouns are: "Sunt itaque genera et species quasi substantiva singularum specierum et generum nomina."[128]

Abelard assimilates universals to the second Aristotelian 'substantiae', which "de subiecto dicuntur" and are not in the subject[129]; they are predicated with the same name and meaning[130] as the individuals[130] (or primary substances) "secundum id quod ex eis unus procedat intellectus"[131], and as Abelard reaffirms, as in the preceding works, that "...nec rem ullam de pluribus dici, sed nomen tantum...", these are clearly terms.[132]

Remembering the terminological difference in the indication of the universal between *Ingredientibus* and *Nostrorum*, it is interesting to see with which appellative Abelard designates the genus of *Dialectica*. The most notable phenomenon here, always within the limits of the section known to us, is the absence of the term 'sermo'[133]; to designate the universal in *Dialectica* the terms 'nomen'[134], 'dictio'[135], 'vocabulum'[136], and above all 'vox'[137] are used. The wide use of this latter confirms Abelard's predilection for this term, which he uses in all four moments of his logical works[138]; it is a term that is pregnant with anti-realistic polemic meaning and is used by the nominalistic tradition from Boetius onwards. Nonetheless, the ambiguity of 'vox' springs into evidence in *Dialectica* as well, where it is also used to indicate what more precisely would be 'materia vocis'.[139]

The second question we can pose about the Abelardian position over the problem of universals, in *Dialectica*, is: what is the meaning of universal nouns?

In this respect the passage already quoted in the previous chapter is the most exhaustive.[140]

Further confirmation is given by a passage of *De Categoricis*.[141] The noun 'homo' is indicated as the same in name and meaning even if one can detect two directions of designation in it: 'circa ad inferiora' and 'ad speciem'. But both as a noun of the individual and as a noun of species it has the same definition, which leads back to an identity of 'impositio'.

Taken as a noun of species – Abelard goes on to say – 'homo' refers to a 'fictio' obtained by 'abstractionem'. We can thus see how the theory of the 'intellectus universalium' of *Ingredientibus* is reconfirmed.

Keeping in mind the development of the discussion in the two already examined texts, another question about the Abelardian conception of universal might thus be formulated: what type of real structure is at the basis of meaning?[142]

The Abelardian attitude concerning the realistic-Platonic doctrine is easily found in a passage of *De locis*.[143] Here the author observes how the opposition of opposites cannot be sustained by the theory of those "qui eandem in essentia materiam generis in omnibus proponunt speciebus ipsis".

The brief exposition of the doctrine and the difficulty met with refer us back quite clearly to the exposition and comment in *Ingredientibus* and *Nostrorum*.[144] The difficulty is heightened by the realism, at times passing to genuses of the other predicaments, for which, according to Aristotelian evidence, there are no specific forms to diversify the identical matter. Abelard thus puts forward his proposal: it is not a question of identity, but of the 'consimilitudo' of essence.[145] This solution is evidently close to the 'convenire in statu' of *Ingredientibus* and to the more generic 'convenientia' of *Nostrorum*.[146]

V

It now remains to consider the various viewpoints from which, naturally with different judgements, the Abelardian position has been seen.

The meaning of the 'res-vox' alternative in which, in Abelard's time, the Porphyrian problem was presented, seems to be the following: the commentator on *Isagoge* and Aristotle, or rather the logician, will develop his inquiry on significant nouns or on the things signified. The opposite position is less dramatic and decisive than it may seem at first sight: several times Abelard has shown how the exclusion of things from the investigation of logic does not deny that they are the basis of the discourse.[147]

The Abelardian position must be considered within these precise historical limits of the alternative: it thus emerges as the most conscious and the most explicitly polemical nominalism. This in fact was what his contemporaries thought.[148]

One has in mind another Occamist nominalism, today, when one judges Abelard as a moderate realist. What, essentially, does one mean by this denomination?

It is certain that one has in mind the Abelardian study of the 'causa communis' as a legitimisation of the meaning of universal nouns, or rather, the theory of the 'status', precisely that whereby Abelard conducted one of the greatest and most openly declared efforts against official realism.

The denomination of 'moderate realism' seems therefore to lack a certain generic quality; it does not strictly define the historical climate of the polemic and furthermore it suggests by this 'moderate' a presumed substitution (in the sphere of the reply to the 'quaestio') of platonising metaphysics by official realism, by a realistic-Aristotelian view which does not seem to be verified in Abelard's case.

The influence of the metaphysical view on the Abelardian solution does not seem to me to transform this into a realistic position for the following reasons:

(a) The 'logical realism'/'philosophical realism' distinction suggested by De Rijk.[149] Abelard was far from saying that universals were reality (however understood), which would be logical realism; he was searching for the basis of the meaning of general nouns in the constitution of 'res';

(b) The 'res', in the case of universals, is not, for Abelard, the indicator but the basis of the value of the meaning (the 'significatio rerum'/'significatio intellectuum' distinction);

(c) On the other hand the study of the real basis of meaning is attenuated in *Nostrorum*, where Abelard insists less on the consideration of the Aristotelian metaphysical conception as determining the value of nouns.

Both Reiners and Geyer[150] have already said there is no basis for the qualification of 'conceptualist'. Their refutation is based on the historical non-existence of an autonomous conceptualist current, and that for Abelard the concept is what is designated and not the universal.

Even if it is too vague and ahistorical, this denomination is nonetheless in a certain sense significative, if one considers the Abelardian conception of 'intelligere' as an intellectual 'actio' directed at the consideration of a 'fictio' or 'similitudo rei'.

For Abelard, the concept contemplated by the mind is an 'imago', a 'figmentum'. In this way, and because this 'figmentum' as a meaning generated by the universal noun is valid, the only criterion that can be assumed seems to be that of a certain 'adaequatio' for the real, an 'adaequatio' which in the case of the universals is incomplete.

It is therefore the Abelardian conception of 'intelligere' that leads Abelard to seek out a real justification for the value of universal nouns; it is his 'conceptualism', if you like, that leads him to 'realism'.

Here, it seems to me, lies the most important distinction between Abelardian nominalism and the nominalism of Occam: the concept of these is no longer the Abelardian 'species' which, given its character, required a confrontation with the real for its validity.

Nevertheless, even with these limitations, Abelard's position in the 'quaestio de universalibus' is important, over and above the explicitly nominalistic statement, for having made the world of nouns and the world of 'res' less directly linked.

This attempt was made possible (even if it does not embark on any definite solution) by the relative autonomy given to 'intelligere': the doctrine of abstraction is at once the conquest and the limit at which Abelard arrived.

REFERENCES

[1] Porphyrius, *Isagoge*, Berlin 1887, p. 25 (10–3).
[2] *G.L.*, p. 3 (18–9).
[3] Porphyrius, *op.cit.*, p. 25 (6).
[4] *G.L.*, p. 3 (21).
[5] *G.L.*, pp. 4 (32), 8 (31), 12 (28), 29 (21), 34 (29), 36 (13).
[6] *G.L.*, p. 22 (6).
[7] *G.L.*, pp. 17, 18.
[8] *G.L.*, p. 31 (19–30).
[9] See also *G.L.*, p. 31 (30).
[10] See Geyer, *op.cit.*, p. 627.
[11] *G.G.*, p. 9 (19–21).
[12] Reiners, *Der Nominalismus in der Frühscholastik*, Munster 1910, p. 52.
[13] As well as 'voces', note 'nomina', already in the formulation of the alternative: *G.G.*, p. 9 (29).
[14] *G.G.*, p. 9 (21ff.).
[15] *G.G.*, pp. 10 (17), 11 (9); the theory seems to result – and the 'teste Boethio' might be a confirmation – from a contamination of the Platonic with the Aristotelian theory: the affirmation of the natural 'subsistentia' of universals refers to the first and more exactly to the conception of the οὐσίαι, while the allusion to the other type of existence ('actualis'), which arises from the occurrence of accidents refers to the Aristotelian power-act distinction.
[16] Abelard, *Ouvrages inédits*, Paris 1836, letter I, c. 2.
[17] *G.G.*, pp. 11–3. Abelard's critical observations will not be specifically expounded here; they are incidentally summed up and paraphrased in Octavian's

work (*Pietro Abelardo*, Rome 1933) and in Vignaux's article ('Nominalisme', in *Dictionnaire de théologie catholique*, Paris 1931).

[18] "...animal formatum rationalitate esse animal formatum irrationalitate": *G.G.*, p. 11 (15). The whole Abelardian argument in this text is a development of these observations, with the exception of the last point in which Abelard observes that if the individuals draw their variety from accidents, these latter must clearly be before the individuals (primary substance). This would mean that the accidents are in neither the individuals nor – and even less so – in the universals (secondary substances whose *raison d'être* resides solely in the primary substances).

This is one of the numerous places where Abelardian terminology reveals a basic adherence to the Aristotelian metaphysical theory (see Geyer, *G.G.*, *Untersuchungen*).

[19] The explicative argument of the 'brunellus' is part of this charge. The procedure of the argumentation is wearisome, the order of the probative propositions being inverted and the conclusion anticipated. This is only one development of the Abelardian observation mentioned at the beginning of note 18 and applies to the individuals the consequences of the affirmed unity of the essence which makes the species undifferentiated. Abelard thus concludes polemically that Socrates is 'burnellus'. We find 'burnellus' in Geyer's edition of *Ingredientibus*. There is no evidence of the use of 'burnellus' in any other Latin text (Du Cange, *Glossarium mediae et infimae latinitatis*, Niort 1885); for this reason I have used the term 'brunellus', which is fairly frequent in the period slightly after Abelard.

[20] *G.G.*, p. 12 (27–31). Standing fast by the same postulate ("eodem tempore tota in singulis") this concerns the consideration of the opposite aspect to that observed by Boetius in an argument against Abelard's 'res generalis' (*G.G.*, p. 31 (1–23)). Boetius observes how the universal, which must be in several existences, loses its own reality. He singles out, namely, the inconvenience that derives from the placing of a universal 'res' by the fact that it loses its existence precisely because of its universality; Abelard, however, points out the reduction of the whole variety of individuals to the single general 'res'.

[21] *G.G.*, p. 14 (1–6).

[22] *G.G.*, p. 14 (7–17).

[23] *G.G.*, p. 14 (18–31).

[24] Prantl reads 'individualiter' and not 'indifferenter'. But the reading 'individualiter' would not point to a movement and a distinction from the identical essence of the first position; it would only indicate the manifestation of the universal in the particular, which is a feature already present in the first formula of realism, if one looks closely at it (Prantl, *Storia della logica in Occidente*, *Età medievale*, Florence 1937, p. 238, n. 104). Gilson (*op.cit.*, p. 293) interprets it as 'indifferenter'.

[25] See the fragment mentioned by Prantl (*op.cit.*, p. 242, n. 108a), which probably belongs to Guillaume de Champeaux.

[26] Prantl, *op.cit.*, p. 262.

[27] Prantl, *op.cit.*, p. 264.

[28] *G.G.*, pp. 14 (32), 15 (22).

[29] *G.G.*, p. 15 (16–8).

30 *G.G.*, pp. 16 (39), 17 (19).

31 *G.G.*, p. 16 (22–35).

32 *G.G.*, p. 136 (31).

33 *G.G.*, p. 18 (6–9).

34 *G.G.*, p. 30 (6–8).

35 *G.G.*, p. 18 (17–20).

36 *G.G.*, p. 19 (21–5).

37 One recalls the "idem totum inesse in pluribus" of the realistic formula, while Abelard uses the expressions 'conveniunt' and 'similes sunt': *G.G.*, p. 19 (23–32).

38 *G.G.*, p. 20 (6–9).

39 *G.G.*, p. 14 (18ff.): "...in eo quod homines sunt ... convenire" and *G.G.*, p. 518 (25ff.): "...aliquis status est participatione cuius multae (substantiae) sunt convenientes."

40 Gilson, however, does so (*op.cit.*, p. 293).

41 *G.G.*, p. 20 (9–12).

42 See Chapter II, n. 14.

43 *Ibidem.*

44 *G.G.*, p. 22.

45 *G.G.*, pp. 20 (18–36), 21 (32).

46 *G.G.*, p. 22 (2–4).

47 *G.G.*, p. 22 (7), 23 (15), 24 (32–7).

48 *G.G.*, p. 513 (16–9).

49 *G.G.*, p. 23 (20–4).

50 *G.G.*, p. 25 (15–25).

51 *G.G.*, p. 25 (29–32).

52 Gilson, *La philosophie au moyen âge*, Paris 1944, p. 287.

53 The distinction of the 'intelligere' and thus of the meaning of a noun from the world of 'res', is, as has already been seen, anything but radical. The expression "...eum qui fallitur non intelligere" with an Anselmian flavour is significant (*G.G.*, p. 322 (1)); here Abelard bases the identity of the 'intellectus' on the identity of the 'res' 'ubicumque', and accentuates the fundamentality in the intellective act of the comprehension of objective reality.

54 This attitude is clearly visible in the discussion of the 'quaestio' of foresight (*G.G.*, p. 27), not so much in the resolution of the problem which repeats the Aristotelian solution (*De Interpretatione*, ed. Minio, p. 19a) as in the awareness that this is one of the cases in which discourse and 'res' cannot coincide.

55 *G.G.*, p. 314 (25–7). This statement follows the denial of the reality of universals and is aimed against the Platonic-realist doctrine which called these forms 'res incorporee' (*G.G.*, p. 314 (14).

56 *G.G.*, p. 317 (3–7).

57 *G.G.*, p. 317 (15–8).

58 *G.G.*, p. 24 (32–7).

59 This might seem to be already evident in the term 'intellectus', with which Abelard indicated the nature of universals as cognitions. However, this term might also have been used in the broad sense, to indicate any type of cognition, even 'opinio' which seems closer to the 'imaginationes' than to the 'intellectus' (*G.G.*, pp. 136–7).

[60] *G.G.*, p. 316 (16).

[61] Contrary to what Gilson says (*op.cit.*, p. 286). Abelard in fact compares it to 'opinio' only with regard to the cognition that God possesses (*G.G.*, p. 23 (11–2)).

[62] *G.G.*, pp. 27 (29), 29 (37). The only noteworthy point seems to me to be the meaning of the term 'significare' on page 29, line 37, which is more unique than unusual. Abelard in fact uses it to indicate both the reference to 'res' (more exactly 'nominatio') and the common 'conceptio'. This seems due to the particular form of the period.

[63] *G.G.*, p. 30 (1–5).

[64] "Non iam permanentibus rosis": in fact the origin of the meaning can always be seen in the 'causa impositionis', or rather in the particular structure of the real (*G.G.*, p. 30 (8)).

[65] *G.G.*, p. 512 (14).

[66] *G.G.*, p. 512 (19–22).

[67] *G.G.*, pp. 514 (32), 515 (9).

[68] *G.G.*, p. 515 (10–3).

[69] *G.G.*, p. 515 (32ff.).

[70] *G.G.*, p. 516 (7ff.).

[71] Gilson, *op.cit.*, p. 280.

[72] *G.G.*, p. 518 (9ff.).

[73] The passage is mentioned by Prantl (*op.cit.*, p. 256, n. 133).

[74] *G.G.*, p. 518 (25–7).

[75] *G.G.*, p. 14 (4).

[76] *G.G.*, p. 19 (21ff.).

[77] Another difficulty for the singling out of those supporting the doctrine of 'convenientia statu' crops up if we bear in mind that Walter de Mortagne presented a theory of the universal understood as 'status' in Paris at this time.

[78] *G.G.*, pp. 518–20. The structure of the passage in question, as often happens in *Nostrorum*, is particularly difficult and asystematic.

[79] *G.G.*, p. 521 (25–9).

[80] *G.G.*, pp. 521 (30), 522 (9).

[81] Prantl, *op.cit.*, p. 262.

[82] *G.G.*, p. 522 (10). Geyer does not point out any lacuna.

[83] This constituted rather a section of particular nominalistic doctrines. Geyer, *op.cit.*, p. 628; Reiners, *op.cit.*, p. 58–9.

[84] Prantl, *op.cit.*, p. 143.

[85] Prantl, *op.cit.*, p. 217.

[86] *G.G.*, p. 513 (15–23).

[87] Bréhier, *op.cit.*, p. 165. This should be left out of consideration in a psychological relation which a realistic theory of universals has with that of archetypal ideas.

[88] *G.G.*, p. 522 (11). This might suggest that the doctrine was new and very personal.

[89] *G.G.*, p. 522 (13–21).

[90] *G.G.*, p. 522. (In *Ingredientibus* Abelard had already guarded against understanding the universal as a physical sound, pointing out that hereby one would fall into the difficulty of realism (*G.G.*, p. 38).)

[91] *G.G.*, p. 38.

[92] *G.G.*, pp. 16 (22), 35, 522 (17).

[93] *G.G.*, p. 32 (2–6).

[94] One should, however, note that also in *Ingredientibus* 'vox' has already been underclassed to indicate the physical sound (*G.G.*, p. 36 (4–7).

[95] Prantl, *op.cit.*, p. 144.

[96] See Geyer, *op.cit.*, p. 627, and Reiners, *op.cit.*, p. 54ff.

[97] *G.G.*, p. 522 (15–6). One must then observe that it would have been more logical, for whoever had examined the text of *De Interpretatione*, to call the universal by a term which gave a better indication of its semantic and non-natural power (see the Abelardian comment on the Aristotelian passage in the *Glosse letterali*: *G.L.*, p. 76). But the Boetian-Roscellian terminology must have contributed to Abelard's solution in *Ingredientibus*. John of Salisbury records Abelard as the supporter of the 'sermo' doctrine (see *Metalogicus*, L. II, c. 17, ed. Webb, p. 92 (1–7).

[98] A residue of the use of 'vox', in the sense of *Ingredientibus*, is also to be found in *Nostrorum*: *G.G.*, p. 537 (7–10).

[99] Unlike Geyer and Reiners, Arnold thinks that Abelard simply pushed the struggle against realism to its limits in his polemic against the 'vox' (*op.cit.*, pp. 58–9). It seems to me that one should bear in mind as well the desire to distinguish his own position from the Roscellian position.

[100] One comes across this statement in *Nostrorum* as well: *G.G.*, p. 524 (32–5).

[101] *G.G.*, p. 525 (2).

[102] *G.G.*, pp. 525 (30), 28 (1).

[103] *G.G.*, p. 525 (32).

[104] *G.G.*, p. 526 (10–3).

[105] *G.G.*, p. 526 (18–21).

[106] Porphyrius, *op.cit.*, p. 1 (9–10).

[107] *Ibidem*, p. 25 (11).

[108] *G.G.*, p. 526 (27–30): "…in statu illo in quo plura participare possunt."

[109] *G.G.*, p. 527 (1–5).

[110] *G.G.*, p. 527 (30–40).

[111] *G.G.*, p. 527.

[112] *G.G.*, p. 528 (9–19).

[113] *G.G.*, p. 528 (30–4). The second part of the Boetian argumentation against the existence of the universal 'res' is openly aimed against the 'collectio' hypothesis, as could already be argued from the hint in *Ingredientibus*. See *G.G.*, pp. 30–1.

[114] *G.G.*, p. 530 (1–15).

[115] *G.G.*, p. 530 (15–20).

[116] *G.G.*, p. 530 (20–5).

[117] *G.G.*, p. 531 (14–9).

[118] *G.G.*, p. 531 (19–20).

[119] *G.G.*, p. 532 (3–8).

[120] *G.G.*, pp. 532 (30), 533.

[121] *G.G.*, p. 540 (10–2).

[122] *G.G.*, p. 23.

[123] This seems confirmed by the difficult form of the exposition.

[124] Abelard, *Dialectica*, Assen 1956, p. XIV. If one thinks that here too Abelard has followed the Porphyrian schema as in the two preceding works, one must add a treatment *De communitatibus*.

[125] Above all the passage in *D.*, p. 112–3.

[126] This deduction is permitted by consideration of the comment on the Porphyrian treatises where, for example, one sees the use of 'res specialis' (*G.G.*, pp. 72–3), which indicates a certain looseness in the terminology when one is outside the systematic exposition of the theory.

[127] *D.*, p. 124 (27–31).

[128] *D.*, p. 321 (15–28); see also *D.*, pp. 538 (36)–9 (1–2).

[129] *D.*, pp. 51 (24–5), 130 (9).

[130] See *D.*, p. 593 (17–26). The same name and meaning is characterised by the unity of 'impositio', whereby a noun is one in matter and meaning (*G.G.*, p. 339). The ambiguity arises from the identity of sound and the difference in the concepts meant (*G.G.*, pp. 117–21).

[131] *D.*, p. 225 (1–3).

[132] *D.*, p. 597 (18–9).

[133] This, however, has little luck in *Nostrorum* either where, in the treatises, we find only 'nomen', 'vocabulum', while 'sermo' belongs only to the formulation of the theory.

[134] E.g., *D.*, p. 112 (32).

[135] E.g., *D.*, p. 115 (1).

[136] E.g., *D.*, p. 65 (15–6).

[137] E.g., *D.*, p. 544 (28).

[138] Even in *Nostrorum*, in the *de genere* treatise (p. 537 (7)) one finds 'voces' with the meaning of 'nomina'.

[139] *D.*, p. 321 (35).

[140] See p. 28.

[141] *D.*, p. 181 (25–37); see also p. 227 (36).

[142] The study of the 'causa communis' through the context of the whole *D.* is perhaps more difficult than others: we must keep in mind that, for the convenience of expression, Abelard will use a terminology that is at times suspect of Platonism. It will be as well to bear in mind the author's statement in *Ingredientibus* (*G.G.*, p. 39 (6–9)), on the need to consider that, in order to construct a science, some properties of nouns do exist.

[143] *D.*, p. 383 (17–84).

[144] The example Abelard gives of the identity of essence 'animalis' in man and ass reveals his attitude of mockery.

[145] *D.*, p. 384 (1–3).

[146] An indirect criticism of realism occurs in a passage from *De divisionibus* (*D.*, p. 575ff.).

[147] This is confirmed in a passage from *Aventinus* (Prantl, *op.cit.*, p. 143, n. 317) which calls the nominalists 'avari rerum', not those denying the real basis, by their demand that logical inquiry deals solely with nouns.

[148] Reiners considers that the Abelardian doctrine is a development of the Roscellian doctrine: *op.cit.*, p. 55.

[149] De Rijk, *op.cit.*, p. cliv.

[150] Reiners, *op.cit.*, p. 54; Geyer, *op.cit.*, p. 628.

CHAPTER IV

THE MEANING OF THE PROPOSITION

At the beginning of the comment on *De Interpretatione* in *Ingredientibus*, Abelard once again stresses that the 'propositio' (a complex but unitary element[1]) is the principal object of the inquiry in question; it is thanks to this that one then examines the noun and the verb as components.[2]

As usual the author starts from the Aristotelian definition of the 'oratio', a complex significative expression; but the points which are of major interest to him are already evident in the illustration.[3] Firstly there is the insistence on the conventional nature of an 'oratio' contrasted with the Platonic conception of the natural quality of the significative phenomenon[4]; then, more notably, the attention to the 'constructio' element of the 'oratio'.[5]

This element, defined as the 'competens coniunctio' of 'dictiones' makes a simple collection of words a true or a false proposal[6], and discriminates between the 'oratio perfecta' and the 'oratio imperfecta'.

This originally grammatical discrimination serves to isolate the 'propositio' by distinguishing it from other complex expressions which affect logic only because they are likely to become subjects and predicates in a proposal of truth.[7]

The concept of the grammatical perfection of a proposition intervenes in the reply to the 'quaestio' on the meaning of the 'enunciatio'.

If the meaning of the proposition was in fact given by the 'res', or by the 'intellectus', the expression 'Socrates currit' would be the same as the expression 'Socrates currens', because 'res' and 'intellectus' are identical in both expressions. One would thus lose the grammatical systemisation of the discourse which provides logic with a precise discriminatory criterion for the various types of complex expressions.[8]

We shall next see how the 'constructio' ideal not only does not coincide (for Abelard) with the ideal of an exact logical construction, but also how a grammatically exact proposition is logically 'incorrect' (this, of course, is quite apart from the 'insignificance' of grammatically correct propositions).

The Abelardian 'sententia' in the comment of *Ingredientibus*, is that the proposition means "id quod proponit et dicit", the 'dictum', and this is the only meaning that assures the statement of its value as a proposal of 'verum vel falsum'.[9]

Holding to the 'dictum' as the meaning of a proposition, one throws light on the unitary and comprehensive nature of an enunciation; the 'res' and the 'intellectus', on the other hand, seem to assure – in a particular way – the validity of the comprehension of the component elements.[10]

The definition of 'dictum' is prevalently negative: its character of 'non-res' and 'non essentia'[11] is stressed (and this is part of Abelard's general aversion to logical realism which is not systematic but continuous), thus denying that the meaning of a proposition is given by its quality that is descriptive of a reality (if one understands 'actual' reality, as we shall see). The 'dictum', however, is not 'nihil'; it is rather affirmed that it is not 'aliquid', or rather that it is not definable in terms of reality.[12]

Abelard seems to point firmly to the purely logical character of the 'dictum' when he notes that "aliud est dicere: non habeo omnem cappam" and "careo omni cappa".[13] The reality 'nominated' is the same: we have reached the antithesis of logical realism.

And the limit of the rôle of 'grammatica' seems clear here: as the language examined is the common conversational language, 'grammatica' commonly understood is what marks the difference between the various types of enunciation, and these differences are nevertheless still 'logically' interesting[14]: not only is the grammatical form different, but the meaning, the 'dictum', is 'aliud'. But this observation is not developed by Abelard in an inquiry within the discourse on the different meaning of the two 'enunciationes'. He seems to be aware of the need for a logical syntax: but if on one hand grammar seems to perform this task, there are, on the other, cases in which 'logical correctness' and 'grammatical correctness' do not coincide.

This seems to happen in a passage from *Categorie*[15]; Abelard distinguishes two ways of considering the meaning of a proposition: the 'discretio animi' and the 'vis significationis'.

The first seems to be the instrument of the inner inexpressed discourse and from habit links the expression 'lego' with the person grammatically copulated with it. In our mind 'lego' is the same as 'ego lego' and is a proposition complete with meaning.

This is not the logician's viewpoint. Compared, in fact, with the 'vis significationis' of the elements of the proposition, the expression 'lego' lacks the indication of the 'substantia' and the 'orationes'; 'lego' and 'ego lego' have different meanings as a result. Up to this point there is, in my opinion, only the concern to exclude from the field of logic any clearly psychological phenomena, such as the mental habit of linking a noun to another which generally goes with it. Abelard says that similar subjective and not strictly determined reasons carry no weight in the examination of the construction of a proposition.[16]

But it seems to me that at a certain point an interesting position (even if it is not developed) is taken up over the 'grammatical' value of an expression.

Compared to 'vis significationis', that is to the logical viewpoint, 'lego' is the same as expressions of the type of 'legis, legit', etc., rather than 'ego lego': the 'sententia' or rather the indication of the meaning is, in fact, 'idem' in all three cases.

Now here it seems to me that the marked indifference for the grammatical form (in this case the conjugation of a verb) in logical inquiry (which is to say, the marked differentiation between the logical and the grammatical value) shows precisely the limits of the role of a grammatical viewpoint in the field of logic. There is, namely, the need for a language 'ultra grammaticam' (in which, for example, the root of a verb accompanied by the personal pronoun replaces the conjugation which may suggest a non-necessity of indicating the person).

Returning to the particular considerations of the 'dictum', we find a precise anti-realistic statement and thus an orientation towards an affirmation of the 'dictum' as 'λεκτόν' in the Stoic sense.

The 'dictum' – it is affirmed – does not come less from 'rebus destructis'. Propositions of the 'hoc non est illud' and 'Socrates est Socrates' type have a value that is independent of the existence of the things nominated (the 'nomen Socrates' on the contrary loses its appellative power 'rebus deletis').[17]

The problem here is considerable: Abelard is aware of the question but does not go into it. It is clear that the two propositions that are party to it are of a particular type: analytical propositions, 'logical truths'. They are not made absolutely true by the 'dictum', but by a particular type of 'dictum'.

In search of a new anti-realistic argument, Abelard points to this type of proposition without indicating its special formal property. For this reason, by propositions of another type, ('Socrates est homo') he is constrained to an acritical indication of the real legitimisation: "nullo modo sine re permanente vera esse potest".[18]

The lack of distinction between the various types of proposition, on the one hand, and the non-existence of a precise definition of the symbols used in the proposition on the other, leads to an interesting, but in some ways not very fruitful, oscillation in the consideration of the value of the 'dictum'.

On the one hand the interest is aimed principally at the expression as such[19] and at times there is the clear-cut statement of the non-existence[20] of a causal link between the reality and the truth of the proposition; on the other there is the acritical return to justification of the realistic type.[21]

The solution to the same 'quaestio' ('de significatione propositionis') is analogously answered in *Dialectica* in a less linear and possibly less mature formulation.[22] The beginning consists of a parallel passage to that in *Ingredientibus*[23]; here he denies that the "significatio veri vel falsi" of a proposition is given by the 'intellectus' which is incapable of ensuring the absolute and permanent necessity for 'consequentia'.

It remains to see if 'verum vel falsum' should be taken as 'nomina propositionis' or 'rerum'. It goes without saying that in the first case one would impose a 'significatio sui' on the proposition, which would be incapable of ensuring the truth of the consequent proposition in the hypothetical case.[24]

Abelard thus attributes the 'significans verum vel falsum' of a proposition to its 'significatio rerum': an expression is true when it proposes 'quod in re est', and false in the opposite case.[25]

Having laid down the criterion for judging the truth of a proposition in the reference to the real plane, Abelard asks himself if the objects "quae a propositionibus dicuntur"[26] are 'res'.[27]

The attitude of this new 'quaestio' already excludes the reply given just above by the tight sphere of a realistic position and makes the same fidelity to the Aristotelian text critical. Taking the same examples of *Ingredientibus*, Abelard excludes the idea that existing things are directly signified by the proposition: this is evident in a certain type of enunciation (tautologies) and in the hypothetical cases, the consecutive need for which survives the destruction of the things 'nominatae'.[28]

The meaning of the propositions would on the contrary be given not by the 'res' directly, but by a "quidam rerum modus habendi".[29]

The proposed solution is terminologically different from that in *Ingredientibus*: it is a matter of seeing if there is also a substantial difference. The two texts are parallel, as we have said, in the way they maintain that the 'intellectus' are not the meaning 'verum vel falsum' of a proposition and conclude that there are no 'res' directly signified by propositions. This last point is raised in different ways in the two texts: we find it as a premise as well as a consideration of the 'intellectus' in *Ingredientibus*[30] and as a specification in *Dialectica*[31] after the statement on the 'significatio rerum' of the proposition.

The most interesting point in *Dialectica* is the absence – in the analogous passage – of the term 'dictum' and of its definitions: in its place one finds "quidam rerum modus habendi".

What is the scope of this expression?

That this is not a matter of an 'actualis' form of reality is evident where Abelard affirms the validity of some propositions 'rebus peremptis'.[32] It would in fact be a question of a 'modus habendi' of 'res' which were also non-existent. And this is in line with Abelard's constant attitude which tends, in several problems, to separate the concept of truth from that of immediate verificability.[33]

To bring the two positions closer – that of *Ingredientibus* and that of *Dialectica* – there is a further affirmation, in the latter text, that the meaning of a proposition is 'in dicendo', not 'in nominando'[34]: the 'dictum' seems to be there in embryo form.

Another analogous element is the importance, in both passages, of the 'constructio' element, which is a necessary condition because it talks of 'significatio'.[35] This introduces the instance of a coherence within the discourse, the first guarantee of meaning.

The lack of a precise formulation of the 'dictum' theory in *Dialectica* accentuates the character whereby an enunciation "de rebus agit"[36]: this in my eyes is the major difference between the two texts.

One should, nonetheless, tread cautiously in stressing this difference, inasmuch as, in *Ingredientibus* as well, recourse to reality as a criterion of the truth of a proposition is anything but absent.[37] In the exposition of *Dialectica* it is apparently possible to see a more immature stage[38] of the Abelardian solution, inasmuch as, even if the attitude remains fundamentally identical, it does not arrive at the proposal and the use of 'dictum', although the elements which agree over its formulation in *Ingredientibus* are already present.[39]

One or two further observations on the Abelardian expression ("rerum modus habendi") in *Dialectica*. Based on a reference by Abelard himself[40], it is possible to connect this to other typical expressions of indubitably metaphysical value ('habitudo rerum'), guaranteeing 'consecutio' and 'in the last analysis', 'significatio'.[41] Quite apart from the existence of any swan, one can always say that "si est cygnus est albus" based on a 'naturae vis inviolabilis'[42], based, namely, quite clearly on a pre-established metaphysically extralogical structure.

Similarly therefore in the discussion of the meaning of the proposition (as earlier in that of the meaning of universal nouns), the most striking point of the Abelardian attitude seems to be its polemical antirealism. This does not seem, here, to take the form of a really positive and new attitude to the problem of meaning. Opposed to this, as we have seen, are a failure to distinguish explicitly between the various types of proposition and a necessary basic realistic guarantee which does not allow a purely extensional reckoning of the elements of the 'propositio'.

In addition, one can attach considerable interest both to the refusal to see a direct link between reality 'actualis' and 'propositio', and to the attention given to the special character of certain propositions (the tautological propositions), the truth of which is based on a value within the proposition itself (or rather on the agreement of the definitions of the terms subject and predicate). One should moreover not forget Abelard's interest in the 'competens coniunctio', in which he tried to see not only the grammatical value.

REFERENCES

[1] The unitary quality of the proposition is deduced from the unity of the 'intellectus', or rather from the unity of the act of comprehension quite apart from the form of expression (which seems on the contrary to determine the *simplicity* of the 'intellectus'). See *G.G.*, pp. 325 (17–37), 326 (16–29).

[2] *G.G.*, pp. 307 (20–3), 207.

[3] *G.L.*, pp. 84–5; *G.G.*, pp. 363–4; *D.*, pp. 146–7.

[4] *G.G.*, p. 363 (25–5); *D.*, p. 147 (11–9). The need to stress this point, which, incidentally, agrees perfectly with the initial definition of logic as the study of significative vocal phenomena 'per impositionem' is inspired from Boetian considerations (*G.G.*, p. 363).

[5] This attitude refers back to Priscian: *G.G.*, p. 364 and *D.*, pp. 148 (19–30).

[6] *G.G.*, pp. 364–5; *D.*, pp. 147–8 (22–8).

[7] *G.G.*, p. 364 (17–21).

[8] *G.G.*, p. 364 (12). Moreover neither 'res' nor 'intellectus', the former possibly disappearing, the latter as 'actiones transitoriae' are capable of ensuring the 'habitudo consecutionis': see *G.G.*, p. 366 (2–12).

[9] *G.G.*, pp. 365 (34–8), 366 (26), 369 (18).

[10] *G.G.*, pp. 367 (9–12), 366.

[11] *G.G.*, pp. 365 (37–8), 366 (27), 368.

[12] *G.G.*, p. 369 (37–8). The 'dictum' as the infallible meaning of a 'propositio' causes truth or untruth: it can perform this function even by not being a 'res': e.g., you die if you have not eaten (*G.G.*, p. 369 (18)). The example is typical of Abelardian anti-realism.

[13] *G.G.*, p. 369 (19–36).

[14] See also: *G.G.*, p. 369 (19–37).

[15] *G.G.*, pp. 137–9.

[16] The same attitude is confirmed in *G.G.*, p. 358.

[17] *G.G.*, p. 366 (27–40).

[18] *G.G.*, p. 366 (32).

[19] See the passage on 'de specie' in *Ingredientibus*: *G.G.*, p. 60 (17–25). Abelard emphasises the need for a view based on the 'vis enuntiationis' rather than on the 'essentia rei'. By this latter 'homo est animal' is false or futile: false if 'animal' is "animal not yet informed about rationality or irrationality"; futile if it is "animal rationalitate informatum". "Ad vim enuntiationis refertur ut videlicet homo *dicatur* esse animal non *sit* animal": hereby the discourse is underlined not as a description of reality but as an enunciation of something. The same elements of reality can be differently discussed precisely on a basis of the diversity of the 'dictum' (*G.G.*, p. 61). This is evident above all in the example: 'aliud est dicere de nullo' and 'aliud est dicere quod nullus...': "qui tacet de nullo dicit, quod currit, nec tamen dicit quod nullus currit..." There is an analogous passage in *D.*, p. 166 (4–15).

[20] *G.G.*, p. 291. Abelard refuses to accept the 'consequentia': "si homo est vera est haec propositio – homo est – "; he notes that the existence of a 'res' in no way determines the construction of a proposition about that 'res'. The 'consequentia conversa' is more interesting: here, having affirmed the truth of 'homo est', he concludes with the existence of 'homo'. Now Abelard denies that one can pass from the affirmation of a truth to a conclusion 'actualis'; he denies the 'consequentia secundum conditionem', that is the causal connexion, which would lead to a strictly realistic position in the 'quaestio de significatione propositionis'; and he accepts the 'consequentia secundum comitationem', that is a reality-truth parallelism which, in logic, cannot be a principle but is a basic guarantee. The 'consequentia secundum comitationem' is, in itself, 'logically' indifferent, but does not hinder a definition of truth which is independent of reality. In this passage a truth-verificability distinction seems to be indicated, though not developed.

[21] *G.G.*, p. 327 (20–1): "enuntiando proponere id quod in re est vel non est in re"; *G.L.*, p. 51 (23–4): "vere gressibile praedicatur de homine quia ita est in re", and also *G.L.*, p. 58 (29–43).

[22] *D.*, pp. 154ff. – See pp. 6–8.

[23] *G.G.*, p. 366 (12–3).

[24] *D.*, p. 156 (1–13). One notes that in the case of 'verum vel falsum' being taken as 'nomina propositionis' one would lose the character of 'nota' which is part of the 'propositio', as it is of the 'nomen' and the 'verbum', and which is the object of logical inquiry, by definition an inquiry into everything that marks something other than itself (*D.*, p. 111).

[25] *D.*, p. 156 (13f.). – Up to this point Abelard is faithful to the Aristotelian attitude.

[26] Note the 'dicuntur' (and not 'nominantur') which in a certain way directs the problem.

[27] *D.*, p. 157 (15–7).

[28] *D.*, pp. 157 (17–31), 160 (14-29); see *G.G.*, p. 366.

[29] *D.*, p. 160 (33–6).

[30] *G.G.*, pp. 366, 367.

[31] *D.*, pp. 154–7.

[32] *D.*, p. 160 (17-21).

[33] See note 20. See also the 'quaestio' on the proposition 'de futuro contingenti': *D.*, pp. 211 (19), 213 (28).

[34] *D.*, p. 140 (22–3). – Bear in mind the value of the 'nominatio'.

[35] *D.*, p. 157 and *G.G.*, p. 369.

[36] *D.*, p. 156; see also *D.*, p. 204 (34).

[37] *G.G.*, p. 327 (20–1).

[38] See p. 6.

[39] In the present state of knowledge of Abelard's works, the 'dictum' theory thus remains typical of the whole *Ingredientibus*. In fact we come across it in the comment on *Categorie*, *De Interpretatione* and *De differentiis topicis* (*G.G.*, pp. 275 (5–6), 327 (20f.); *G.L.*, pp. 225 (39), 226 (16)). Likewise in the section of the comment on *De Interpretatione* published by Minio Paluello one finds the expression 'dictum propositionis': see p. 15 (18), *op.cit.*

This (as well as other characteristic positions such as the universal 'vox' theory and the distinction between 'vox' and 'materia nominis') seems of great significance for acknowledging that *De differentiis topicis* belongs to *Ingredientibus*.

[40] Pointed to by De Rijk: *D.*, pp. 264 (38), 282 (25).

[41] From a passage in *De locis* one can see the metaphysical value of this 'natura' or 'habitudo rerum' (even if Abelard then switches his interest to the consequent 'natura' or 'habitudo terminorum'), where it is opposed to the 'complexio' of what, on the contrary, is the logical value (*D.*, p. 256 (20f.).

[42] *D.*, p. 283 (12–3).

CHAPTER V

THE 'ARGUMENTATIO'

The study of the connections of the propositions in the 'argumenta-tio' is the last step of a series of more particular inquiries which make up the tissue of the science of logic: in two parallel passages in *Ingredientibus* and *Nostrorum*[1] Abelard has clearly underlined the path of the 'discretio argumentandi', which is frequently denounced in his anti-rhetorical scientificity.

The 'argumentatio' is the aim of dialectics and the importance of an examination of the instruments whereby the 'argumentationes' are constructed thus comes to the forefront: syllogisms and 'loci'.

The syllogism in its dual Boetian capacity of categorical and hypothetical syllogism is studied by Abelard in *Dialectica* in the third book of the second treatise and in the second book of the fourth treatise.

But to judge by a precise reference in *Ingredientibus* as well to a treatment *De Hypotheticis*[2], Abelard must have examined the main instrument of the 'argumentatio', and certainly in its categorical capacity, as can be deduced from three indications[3] (even if none of them are very precise). But the actual order which Abelard follows in his comments authorises us to think that there must have been a complete treatment of syllogisms in his notes.

The 'auctoritas' to which Abelard refers in *Dialectica* is, as usual, Aristotle, but he closely follows the work of Boetius[4], as can be seen from the numerous references. Abelard starts from the Aristotelian definition of syllogism, which was also accepted by Boetius: "syllogismus...oratio est in qua positis aliquibus aliud quid a positis ex necessitate consequitur ex ipsis esse...."[5] By a systematic illustration of this definition, Abelard distinguishes the syllogism from other verbal expressions[6] and stresses the perfection of the syllogistic 'complexio', whence issues the need for the conclusion.[7]

It does not appear, however, that Abelard is disposed to consider that a syllogism is a 'complexio', the premises of which are not true: the syllogism is valid argument, also because from the start the 'assumpta' assure the presence of a guarantee of extralogical order[8], and also because reality is constructed syllogistically. But this last point causes what had already happened in other delicate and crucial logical questions, such as the problem of meaning or, more generally, the inquiry into the concept of logic and its differentiation with regard to metaphysics: this, basically, is an element that is foreign to the material which Abelard then handles, from the moment when it becomes clear from his inquiries that the syllogism interests him above all in a quite different, and namely in a more rigorously formal, aspect (as had similarly occurred for the 'significatio' as distinct from the 'nominatio').

There is no shortage of precise Abelardian statements on this last point: on the perfection of the syllogism quite apart from the truth of the component propositions[9]; on its necessity and indubitability.[10] All these statements imply an implicit distinction between the truth of the syllogism (and the concept of truth, as has been seen, is still metaphysically compromised in Abelard) and 'necessitas' or 'perfectio' or 'indubitabilitas' (the Abelardian terminology, usually so precise, wavers here without any clear distinction of formal or psychological criterion). This attitude arises in another passage from *Dialectica*: "Sive veris propositionibus sive falsis, syllogismus texatur dunmodo formam teneant syllogismi, tota tamen ipsius inferentia firmissima semper erit." It is significant that this statement belongs to the treatment of hypothetical syllogisms from the moment when the hypothetical proposition, for Abelard, is precisely one of those cases in which the thing-discourse break appears deepest and clearest.[11] With regard to the perfect character – from the logical viewpoint – of the syllogistic 'complexio', Abelard returns to the text *De Locis* and observes that the terms of the syllogism are not to be considered designative of reality but rather as elements of a calculation: in fact, in order to be perfect 'inferentiae'[12], syllogisms need neither the 'habitudo rerum' (with a clear metaphysical flavour) nor the 'habitudo terminorum' (a typical expression of compromise that brings a guarantee of extralogical order to the sphere of logic).[13] This type of consideration might allow the possibility of translating the Abelardian syllogistic schema into a formula of implication, i.e. of transforming this typical Aristotelian instrument, modelled implicitly on a determined metaphysical hypothesis, into an effective instrument, but a rigidly formal one, and verifiable for any value of the terms. De Rijk apparently thinks that this transformation is authorised by certain attitudes and statements of Abelard himself.[14] And first of all he quotes an Abelardian passage where the Master declares that the syllogism can be considered a hypothetical proposition. But to redimension the value of this position there is a passage in *De Differentis topicis* in *Ingredientibus*: Abelard here calls the 'sententia' whereby the syllogism is a hypothetical proposi- tion 'communis', and traces it back to Boetius ("est quidem com- munis sententia et syllogismum et omnem argumentationem esse hypotheticam propositione").[15] The problem, as I see it, does not reside in the translation of the Abelardian formulae of the syllogism into logical formulae of implication, taking the cue from certain suggestive statements made by Abelard[16], but rather in fixing the Palatine Master's position in this respect, as has already been done for the other problems, historically, and in recording the uncer- tainties in the definitions of the most interesting logical concepts. It is true that Abelard calls the premises of the syllogism 'propositio' and 'assumptio' and that the rules of many syllogisms have the form of an implication, but the value of these statements is measured and laid down in the conception of the syllogism as such. But what is the syllogism for Abelard? His attitude is a dual one in this res- pect (which is why it is interesting and liable to future develop- ments): on the one hand there is the clear aproblematic statement (the more notable for being implied) that the syllogism is a scientific instrument because it is based on the truths of the 'assumpta' and that the syllogism is a conjecture, but a particular one, guaranteed 'from the outset'; on the other, both in the determination of the syllogistic rules and in other positions taken up with regard to the validity of the conjectures (which, when freed from the relation with reality, must be studied and appraised on a basis of the necessity of their 'consecutio' and not of the meaning of the two component parts), as, incidentally, in the already quoted passages on the formal perfection of the syllogistic inference, Abelard shows his heart to be more in the inquiry into the formal aspect of the syllogistic calculation than in the metaphysical guarantee of its truth. When all is said and done it seems that the modern concept of implication is – as, incidentally, is normal in logic of Aristotelian derivation – foreign to the Palatine Master's position: the 'antecedens' and the 'consequens' of the conjectures are connected by relations in meaning and not by relations among values of truth.

As far as Abelard's position is concerned, the most interesting aspect is lost in a syllogism-implication identification: the wavering between two opposed positions, the traditional and implicit position of plainly Aristotelian derivation, whereby the syllogism is an instrument of truth which is not strictly formal and which is complicated in the problem of meaning by extralogical elements, and the so-to-speak newer and more rigorous position whereby it becomes a calculation whose absolute logical purity is frequently emphasised by Abelard. The first reason, indeed, when all is said and done, remains implicit in the particular inquiry on the various forms and shapes of the syllogism it is omitted, while the second constitutes the whole framework of the author's dialectic research.

The illustration of the shapes and ways of the syllogism closely follows the Boetian exposition.[17]

In the treatise De syllogismis categoricis we find a brief note which is of help with regard to the observations that can be made on the theories of inherence and identity in Abelard.[18] As De Rijk[19] has observed, it seems that, in Dialectica, Abelard rejects the theory of inherence for that of the identity of predicate and subject: and, as emerges from a passage of De Locis, the theory of inherence is more compromised metaphysically by the insistence in the last analyis that there is an 'inhaerentia rerum' of the predicate and the subject at the basis of the copulation of the verb to be, which makes the enunciation valid.[20] But Abelard observes the difficulty that would occur for hypothetical propositions and for the application of the 'maximae propositiones' to the 'loci', just as in *Ingre-dientibus* he had had to resort to a distinction (of an extralogical order) between inherence 'in adiacentia' and 'in essentia' to explain the proposition 'Socrates est albus'.[21] The theory of identity, on the contrary, proposes an identification of the significative spheres of the subject and the predicate which can also be justified from a purely logical viewpoint. To this effect, Abelard notes in the treatise *De syllogismis categoricis* that his use of the terms 'predicari' and 'removeri' is parallel to the Aristotelian 'inesse' and 'non inesse' because of the greater adherence to the terminology on the part of his contemporaries. It seems clear that the theory of inherence, as formulated in *Ingredientibus*, is henceforth dropped in the face of the need for a more precise determination of the logical criterion that directs the inquiry: this need is all the more interesting because, from Abelard's words, it seems to involve a phenomenon which is not only personal but common to the other dialecticians of the time.

To date we have two Abelardian texts concerning the definition and the description of the various types of 'loci': one is in the form of a comment, the other in the form of an autonomous exposition, and both are guided by the Boetian text *De Differentiis topicis*.[22]

In both texts the definition of 'locus' is the Boetian one of 'argumenti sedes'.[23] In *Dialectica* Cicero's definition of 'vis inferentiae'[24] is proposed.

It is evident from both definitions what position 'locus' occupies in the general picture of the 'scientia logica', constituting one of the instruments suited to the 'inventio' of the argumentations.[25]

There is an immediate problem here: where do the 'loci' derive their capacity of 'inferentia' and in what are they distinct from the syllogisms? Abelard makes a precise statement with regard to this: the 'locus', consisting of a single antecedent and a consequent, does not have that perfection of 'complexio' that made the syllogistic calculation constantly true, beyond the truth of its components. The characteristic of the inference of the 'loci' compared to the syllogism is clearly indicated in the wide and explicit considerations of *Dialectica* as well as in the comment: there are argumentations, Abelard says, which derive their 'vis inferentiae' from the 'proprietas terminorum' and from the 'constructio', and others from the 'natura rerum'.[26] Another clear statement in this respect is to be found in the text of *Nostrorum*: some argumentations are 'complexionales', that is, they accept the need from the 'dispositio terminorum', and others, the 'locales' from the 'proprietates sermonorum' and from the 'eventus rerum'.[27] With the considerations of *Dialectica* as a basis, we can single out the syllogism in the first type of 'argumentatio'; for the second the reference to the 'loci' is explicit. The imperfection of construction of the 'locus' compared with the syllogism must be replaced, because the need for consequence is maintained by another element, and Abelard indicates this in his consideration of the designated value of the terms used in the topical argumentation (irrelevant in the syllogism from the viewpoint of the 'perfectio inferentiae'): or rather in the constancy of the significative sphere of words ('habitudo terminorum') which is based on a 'habitudo rerum' or 'natura rerum'.[28]

Consideration of the metaphysical plane thus also finds its way into this inquiry on the 'loci' and, as usual, has the task of guaranteeing the basis of the discourse; the 'natura rerum' is the eternal regularity of the world[29], the order of things which the dialectician presupposes but does not use in his exclusively logical research.

The 'locus' is only probable; it is not true (and thus concerns the rhetorician and not the logician[30]) when, at the basis of a 'habit' of terms, there is a certain constancy detectable in the occurrences of actual things, a certain preponderance of events which are analogous to the proposal in the 'locus'[31]; it is true, on the other hand, when the terms of the topical calculation are connected by a bond expressed in a proposition with a universal character, the 'maxima propositio'. Abelard accepts the Boetian definition[32] and stresses the indemonstrability of these rules which are analogous to the rules of mathematics and grammar.[33] The comment here uses a more rigorous terminology than that in *Dialectica*: the 'maxima propositio' is a 'propositio' "per se nota, id est ex propria inventione... certa sicut... quaecumque regulae" and the author does not hint that they have a truth of a metaphysical order but rather suggests an interesting evaluation of these logical truths which would have the same function and the same structure as the analytical propositions of present-day formal logic. With regard to the 'locus differentia' as well we find a more precise definition in the comment: "Ille est qui a termino ducitur questionis hoc est qui assumitur in argumentatione ad probandam questionem de habitudine per quam recipit terminum questionis...", while in *Dialectica* we have "ea res in cuius habitudine ad aliam firmitas consecutionis consistit".[34] Here there is a difference which is clearly only terminological, but the rigour present in the treatment of the comment is interesting, conveying, as it does, a definition which is already loaded with metaphysical suggestions on to an exclusively sermonical plane. In conclusion: in this inquiry, likewise, the Abelardian attitude is not dissociated from the typical attitude. On the one hand we do not feel authorised to load Abelard's statements about the indemonstrability of the 'maximae propositiones' with a 'modern' meaning, but, according to the text, we have to maintain the basic metaphysical guarantee; on the other it is evident that the Abelardian procedure in this field can, on the contrary, be likened, in practice, to that of a present-day logician: for the construction of an argumentation an analytical *a priori* true rule is called for, through the 'locus differentia', namely the analysis of the type of term to be used.

Likewise in the more significative 'quaestio' of the two 'de locis' treatments we find a rigorous and critical position in the comment, which suggests a later drafting than that of the parallel passage in *Dialectica*.[35]

The 'quaestio' pivots on the problem whether the 'maxima propositio' should also involve "de rebus... per voces", in order to sustain the 'loci differentiae' which, like all propositions, involve 'de rebus'. Opposed to this is the fact that in the 'maxima propositio' there is a universal type of enunciation and it is therefore not possible to sustain that this involves a 'res universalis' given that "secundum nostram sententiam solae voces universales vel particulares per apposita signa proponi possunt".[36] One solution would be: to consider the 'maxima propositio' as a 'regula multiplex' containing all the 'loci' where it is at the basis, which would mean saying, for example, that the term 'species' in a 'maxima propositio' means all the individual species.[37] But it suffices here to recall how Abelard insisted on the 'nominatio-significatio' distinction and made his consequent statement about the unity of meaning of universal nouns. "Nobis tamen non placet haec multiplicitatis sententia..."[38]; it is natural that Abelard should also confirm on this occasion that a universal noun signifies 'indeterminates' and does not refer to individuals.[39] His proposed solution is consequent with his other attitudes: the 'maxima propositio' states relations between nouns (like 'genus' and 'species') which allows the 'assignatio loci differentiae'[40]: in fact to demonstate the evidence of an argumentation reference is made to the 'locus' which is basically "veluti cum dicimus; locus est a specie". In this expression and in the enunciation of the 'maxima propositio' ("de quibusdam predicatur species et genus") genus and species are taken to be 'nomina vocum', which allows the 'maxima propositio' to be really at the basis of the particular 'locus' in question.

The situation in *Dialectica* is quite different and the upsetting of the statements could not be more surprising.

If in the comment Abelard expressly refuses 'haec multiplicatis sententia', here he says that the 'maximae propositiones' should be considered 'consequentiae multiplices'[41] because they contain 'in sensu suo' all the 'loci differentiae' of which they are the basis; if in the comment he says he prefers the categorical to the conditional form, in *Dialectica* he indicates that the more precise expression for the 'maxima propositio' is precisely this latter.[42] The basic difference is the clear and aproblematic statement that the 'maximae propositiones' involve 'de rebus'.[43] Even when he unfolds the discussion of the 'quaestio' Abelard again covers the same points and reverses his statements: in *Dialectica* he says that the reflexive pronoun makes a universal proposition 'multiplex', like 'omnis res predicatur de se'. This is the same as: 'Socrates est Socrates', 'Plato est Plato', etc.[44]; in the comment there is a plain refusal of this equivalence.[45] Such a systematic contradiction can only mean a punctilious self-revision of his own positions, but in what chrono-logical order? The attitude of the comment is, on the whole, more critical and thus more mature, presupposing a contrary position, forestalling the objections, and clarifying the difficulties; the attitude in *Dialectica*, on the contrary, is acritical and lacks the broad view of discussion which occurs in the note. As we have seen, the position of the comment is in addition in line with Abelard's most original attitude; which emerges above all from the extensive notes in *Ingredientibus*. But there is another element which strengthens the hypothesis of a chronological priority, as far as this passage is concerned, of the treatment in *Dialectica* on the comment *Super Topica*: the presence in these pages of an example which by its character ('Petrum diligit sua puella') indicates, as D'Olwer has observed, that the drafting of this section goes back to before 1118. Our investigation into the inner characteristics of this passage simply confirms, and strongly in my opinion, that certain parts of *Dialectica* were written before the composition of *Ingredientibus*: D'Olwer's observations, which held that the *Ingredientibus* came before all the drafts of *Dialectica*, agree perfectly with the results of this analysis because they confirm that the passage in question is among those which belong to the earliest drafting.

REFERENCES

1 *G.G.*, pp. 2 (8ff.), 508.
2 *G.G.*, p. 309 (7).
3 *G.G.*, pp. 394 (10–26), 487, 499 (24ff.).
4 See De Rijk, *op.cit.*, p. xix.
5 *D.*, p. 232 (4–10).
6 *D.*, pp. 232, 233.
7 *D.*, p. 233 (6).
8 *D.*, p. 232 (21); *G.L.*, pp. 321 (25)–2 (1); *D.*, 254 (531ff.).
9 *D.*, p. 233 (6).
10 *D.*, p. 255 (36–7).
11 *D.*, p. 499 (30).
12 *D.*, pp. 256 (34), 257 (24ff.); *D.*, pp. 253–4, 255 (32).
13 *D.*, p. 255.
14 De Rijk, *op.cit.*, pp. xxxii–xxxiii.
15 *G.L.*, pp. 321–2.
16 See also *D.*, p. 471 (31), 282–3, 271.
17 *D.*, pp. 234–49; Boetius, *P.L.*, p. LXIV.

18 *D.*, p. 239 (20–7).
19 De Rijk, *op.cit.*, pp. xxxviii–xxxix.
20 *D.*, p. 329 (19ff.).
21 *G.G.*, pp. 360–1.
22 *G.L.*, pp. 205–330; *D.*, pp. 253–413.
23 *G.L.*, p. 206 (33); *D.*, p. 253 (22).
24 *D.*, p. 253 (16).
25 *G.L.*, pp. 213, 319 (16–8). In the comment this is explicitly stated on the guidance of the Boetian text (Boetius, *P.L.*, pp. LXIV, 1173–84) and the general considerations on logic and its ramifications are repeated. In an autonomous treatment such as *Dialectica* this type of consideration was to be found *una tantum* at the beginning of the text.
26 *G.L.*, p. 309. The 'proprietates terminorum', together with the 'constructio' can be interpreted as 'complexio terminorum'.
27 *G.G.*, p. 508 (9–15). The 'proprietates sermonum' are different from the 'terminorum'; with the first the value of the word is indicated as significative; with the second it is alluded to as an element of the whole expression.
28 *D.*, pp. 256–7.
29 Distinct herein from the 'actus rerum': see *D.*, pp. 282 (30–7), 265.
30 *D.*, p. 274 (28–9).
31 *D.*, p. 271 (35ff.): "Sunt autem quidam qui non solum necessarias consecutiones sed quaslibet quoque probabiles veras esse fateantur." Among these 'quidam' Abelard indicates a 'Magister Noster' whom De Rijk, somewhat doubtfully, interprets as Guillaume de Champeaux. But Abelard himself indicates that at the basis of this 'sententia' there is a clearly subjectivistic and not 'realistic' criterion ("probabilitas ad visum referenda est, veritas autem sola ad rei existentiam"), and this viewpoint seems rather alien to a realist like Guillaume. See the clear example of probable 'locus' on p. 277 (333ff.); in the following lines note the fairly rare meaning (in Abelard) of 'dialecticus' as rhetorician, swiftly followed by the normal meaning of 'dialecticus'=philosopher.
32 *D.*, p. 263 (11).
33 *G.L.*, pp. 207 (1), 230 (3ff.), 244 (32).
34 *G.L.*, p. 207 (4); *D.*, p. 263 (7).
35 *G.L.*, p. 238 (35ff.); *D.*, p. 317 (2ff.).
36 *G.L.*, p. 235 (10).
37 *G.L.*, p. 235 (22).
38 *G.L.*, p. 235 (26).
39 *G.L.*, p. 235 (31).
40 *G.L.*, p. 239 (20ff.).
41 *D.*, p. 317 (23).
42 *D.*, p. 317 (28–9).
43 *D.*, p. 267 (25ff.).
44 *D.*, p. 318 (26ff.).
45 *D.*, p. 235 (28ff.). See also the expression 'exprimens habitudinem vocum' referring to the definition of 'maxima propositio' (*G.L.*, p. 239 (36)), while in *Dialectica* we find on several occasions the expression 'habitudo rerum' (e.g. p. 256).

APPENDIX: *ABAELARDIANA INEDITA*

The text *Sententie secundum Magistrum Petrum* published by Minio and Paluello in *Abaelardiana inedita* is attributed by him to Abelard on the basis of various considerations: the presence of the appellative 'Magister Petrus', a denomination which we find applied only to Abelard in this period; the distinction between 'ad sensum' and 'personalis' signification which is typical of Abelard; the use of certain examples which are already present elsewhere in the works of the Palatine Master; and an inexact reference to Boetius already repeated in *Ingredientibus*.[1] With regard to the style, Minio finds nothing in this text which can be easily shown to be alien to Abelard's style: in my opinion there is, however, a certain difference, which complicates the comparison, between the type of freer and less restricted discourse of these *Sententie* and the discourse of the other works. As for other evidence, it seems to me that one should take note that the distinction between 'significatio ad sensum' and 'personalis' is contained in the other Abelardian works but with a different terminology[2], while the use of various examples common to *Ingredientibus* might not be of particular significance. In fact the liveliness of the polemics which were then brewing among dialecticians created a common language and a need to refer to points that were immediately comprehensible. Minio's considerations do however suggest that a wider examination of the content of these *Sententie* would be useful; such an examination would throw light on the attitudes and expressions which could most clearly be assimilated to the Abelardian position.

In his analysis of the paralogism[3] and in his confutation of the syllogism, "hic homo est hoc corpus, sed hoc corpus est prius hoc homine, ergo hic homo est prius hoc homine", the author keeps the plane of the 'significatio' in mind, which coincides with the plane of the 'intellectus'[4] by following a classically Abelardian procedure. In order to maintain the 'complexio' of the syllogism, reference is made not so much to the meaning as such, but to the persistence of a constant significative plane throughout the 'argumentatio'. It is precisely here that the author focusses his criticism: the perfection of the 'complexio argumentationis' (a typically Abelardian term) is based not on the reference to the plane of reality or on the 'significatio rerum', but on the identity of value of the symbol in the three phases of the syllogism (an identity which is not respected in the paralogism because the modal determination of the 'assumptio'[5] is "ita quod hoc corpus posset esse absque hoc homine", while in the conclusion we have "ita quod hic homo posset esse absque hoc homine").[6] Likewise the modification of the 'argumentatio' (and this procedure is also typically Abelardian, or rather the impartial analysis at the basis of the argumentations which are in opposition precisely owing to their more complete confutation)[7] is not accepted by the author because the general rule which could be induced – which is a 'simple' enunciation and does not contain modal determinations – is not adjusted to it. Furthermore, and this is the most interesting point for the comparison that can be made with passages which are definitely Abelardian, there is a definition with regard to this in the *Sententie* of 'significato personalis' which recalls the definition of 'significato rei' in *Ingredientibus*, which is moreover made with reference to a passage from Priscian on the transitive and intransitive 'coniunctio', and is clearly used in *Dialectica* as well.[8] Lastly a warning from the author, which is noteworthy for its analogy with the Abelardian attitude: "magis sensum quam verba pensemus", recalls the constant consideration of the significative plane compared to a Roscellinian brand of nominalism.[9] The Abelardian echoes are thus all the more interesting because they are conceptual, not terminological: the alertness of the Palatine Master's thought led him in fact more than once to a change of language in his search for a more precise position: the attribution of a text to Abelard can be made more on the basis of a productive intellectual fidelity to an attitude than on the basis of a rigorous coherence and persistence of language which, all things considered, is sterile. Now, we find this fidelity in this passage as well, in the strictly sermonising attitude which is nonetheless attentive on the plane of meaning as a guarantee of the value of the argumentations.

Again from the viewpoint of identifying the author of *Sententie*, examination of the 'de toto' sophisms can be of greater interest once it is possible to refer to passages from *Ingredientibus* and *Dialectica*.

The five difficulties over the relation between 'totum' and 'pars' are raised first and foremost by those "qui totum solummodo vocem esse confitentur"[10] against what I should say is a plainly realistic interpretation. This, say the nominalists, leads to nonsenses. It suffices to illustrate the first: if[11] 'in rebus conspiciamus' it is not true that six consists of four and half of four because there is no number four which 'per se' can form a six by the addition of its half, if there is not *another* two to add. The repetition of analogous expressions ("si rem ex re constare dicamus", "secundum constitutionem rei")[12] clearly indicates the characteristic of the opposing position which seems to hold to a rigid realism: in any case we can say that, perhaps by polemical facility, their position is anything but elastic, indeed it is rather in a rigorous observance of the plane of things. The suspicion about an alternative polemic is also justified by that 'nos' ("nos impugnare posse videtur")[13] at the beginning, which would tend to indicate those accused by the nominalists. Whoever the author of *Sententie* is, it is evident that his critical and shrewd position is considerably more articulate than the showing of the opposition would have one suppose.

In the solution of the first sophism ('de senario') the author's attitude is not in defence of the realist viewpoint and is thus between the two positions, the acritical nominalistic (one is tempted to say Roscellinian) and the realist, as presented by the opponents. It is not by suggestion that we call this type of attitude Abelardian: as we shall see more particularly in examining the last sophisms, Abelard more than once takes a discriminating position between the two texts, realist and Roscellinian, on the line of one and the same informatory principle.[14] This is also easy to see in this solution and precisely in the distinction between two 'powers' of meaning of the words: 'secundum personam' and 'secundum speciem'.[15] The first is a 'significatio discreta', the second 'indifferenter'. This latter has its 'causa impositionis' in the 'identitas naturae' or rather in the 'convenientia' or 'similitudo rerum'. As for the two types of 'significatio', we find the expression 'personaliter' applied to the 'significatio distincta' of a noun, while the reference to the general concept is called 'confuso' and 'indeterminato'[16] in a text which is definitely by Abelard. But an even more complete and convincing analogy is to be found in the treatment of universals in *Ingredientibus* and *Nostrorum*, as emerges from the examination carried out in Chapter III. In the short passage from *Sententie* we find, namely, both the elements which, in my opinion, have characterised the Abelardian position in the problem of meaning of general nouns: the indication that the qualification of universal or particular of words lies in the type of significative 'vis', together with the admission (more wary, as we have seen, in *Nostrorum* than in *Ingredientibus*) of the existence of a justification in the plane of things, in their 'similitudo' or 'convenientia'.

The distinction between the two types of signification (a distinction which is impossible for a realist of the type to whom the sophism is applied and which is alien to a 'Roscellian' nominalism)[17] allows the author to demonstrate the erroneous nature of the argumentation in which the nominalist makes use of the same word and does not notice the change of 'significato'.[18]

In the second and third difficulties posed by the nominalists the author has an easy task; he opposes it with a more subtle analysis of the significative sphere.[19]

More interesting for the Abelardian cross-references is the 'solutio' to the last two difficulties. These concern the noun 'totus' which, loaded with a strict realistic signification, raises difficulties which are like those over universals: according to the real plane ('secundum constitutionem rei') one cannot define the expression 'si domus est, paries est' 'locus a toto' because the individual things (this house) cannot prove the existence of other things (this wall).[20] In the presentation of the difficulty against which the realists run up we can already observe an interesting element which in a precise way determines the opposing positions: the nominalists, in indicating the absurdity of a real justification of the 'locus a toto' admit that this is a matter of resorting to 'res individue' on the part of the realists and not of universal realities once "universalia...vocabula ad nullam subiectarum rerum percipiendam nos dirigunt".[21] It seems clear that this is not the point to be discussed, but the reference to individual things: a 'Platonic' realism is thus neither taken into consideration nor attributed by the nominalists to their opponents in the dispute. This would show that the platonising realism of Guillaume de Champeaux 'prima maniera' was a fairly limited fact: Guillaume's withdrawal, the lack of precise evidence of Platonic realism except for Anselm's statements, the abundance, on the contrary, of the evidence of Abelard and John of Salisbury of more 'moderate' realist theses, all this seems to indicate that the opposition between nominalists and realists had a wider and more generic bearing (even if no less fundamental) than the 'de generibus' dispute taken on its own might have one suppose. The problem of universals was a sharpening of a larger and more important problem which questioned the value and function of logic: the justification of the value of an 'argumentatio' (which is the 'locus') is included here.

The difficulty is overcome by the author through the assumption of a very precise position: "hanc vocem totum locum esse proprie concedimus non significatum ipsius."[22] This is a decidedly nominalistic position, but as the preceding pages have shown in the polemic with the nominalists it is distinct from a 'Roscellinian' type of position which is critically militant. The statement is in fact based on the consideration that only the purely logical plane (the 'significatum' of the above-quoted passage is evidently a 'significatum rei') is able to provide a precise discrimination between the 'loci differentiae'. According to the plane of things, in fact, the 'maximae propositiones', nominating the same 'res', would not be differentiated and thus it would come about that there would be no difference between a rule stating relations 'a genere' and one 'a toto'.[23] The author, however, says that the distinction is precisely 'in nominibus tantum'. In this respect our examination is helped by a passage from the Abelardian *Dialectica* which concerns the same problem.[24] Like the author of *Sententie*, Abelard also says that the 'loci differentiae' are less numerous than the 'maximae proposi- tiones' on the basis of the consideration that although the things nominated are identical (e.g. the 'res homo') and the 'relatio' is different (e.g., 'ab opposito' or 'a specie'), there are two different 'differentiae'; in turn "eadem differentia diversas habeat maximas propositiones" as the 'modus inferentiae' is different (this too being an exclusively logical element as one can see from the three examples given by Abelard).[25] The position of the author of *Sententie* is analogous to that of Abelard precisely because for both it is exclusively in the plane of the predication that the sense and bearing of logical classifications, which would be annulled according to the plane of things, should be looked for.

Still like our author, Abelard refers back to the Boetian passage in which – in order to give a better explanation of what is meant by 'locus differentia' – one can see the analogy passing between the specific difference ('rationalitas') and the 'locus differentia maximae propositionis'.[26]

As for the statement by our author that one should refer the 'locus' to the exclusively vocal plane, one may recall here how, in *Super Topica*, Abelard insisted, as we have seen, on the sermonising sphere both of the 'locus differentia' and of the 'maximae proposi- tio'.

One can also mention another Abelardian passage: it belongs in *Dialectica* and deals with the 'divisio totius'.[27] Here too Abelard seems to choose a more critical and articulate attitude, just as he did in the 'quaestio de universalibus', from the two positions: the realist and the 'insana' of Master Roscellin. He reproaches the realists for not discriminating between the principal and the se- condary part due to their pedestrian consideration of the plane of things in which it happens that every part is equally necessary for the existence of the 'totum', thus obstructing a 'divisio totius' on the logical plane. On the other hand there is the 'insana sententia' of Roscellin who says that 'pars' is only a 'vox' and defends his statement with the following sophism: if one says that the 'res' house consists of other 'res' (walls and foundations), one ends up saying that the 'res' wall, a part of the 'res' house, because the latter is no more than walls, roof, and foundation, is at once part of itself and part of the other walls.[28]

Abelard's attitude is neither so explicit nor so clear as that taken in the 'quaestio de generibus': in the 'perfectio totius'[29] he implies the criterion for establishing whether a part is principal or secondary and in this way indicates those parts which, in conjunction, produce (evidently not 'in re' but according to the conceptual significative plane) a complete totality as happens for the house with the roof, walls, and foundations as the principal parts. He then quickly adds, however, that (and he uses the expression "si rei veritatem confiteamur") one should never talk of 'tota temporalia' once the supposed parts of these never exist 'simul'. But it is an intellectual element that makes him call them 'tota': 'secundum considerationem' in fact they are 'accepti' as 'tota'.[30] The criticism on Roscellin provides a further specification of the Abelardian position: the master's sophism is invalidated by saying that the 'totum' (the house) is not the sum of the parts but the union of them "simul accepta et coniuncta".[31] As can be seen, this is a matter of generic statements (one could say hesitant), almost in search of a criterion that flees the difficulties of a plainly realistic position and the difficulties of Roscellinian 'vocalism', without any very precise and rigorous formulation.[32] In the short passage in *Sententie* about the 'divisio totius' the author had faced the same problem of discrimination between secondary and principal part, and resolved it in a similar way: when one says that 'house' is divided 'sufficienter' among walls, roof, and foundations, one means that these three parts contain, by constitution, all the others (bricks, plaster, etc.).[33]

To conclude this brief examination, it seems to me that, first of all, one should bear in mind that the argument of these *Sententie* is not particularly favourable to the analysis aimed at detecting in them an Abelardian attitude: we have in fact seen how Abelard does not appear clear and precise in his positions in the analogous passages of the works already known to us. Essentially, while a treatment 'de universalibus' or on the signification of the 'propositio' could be more easily attributed to Abelard given that the language on these occasions is rigorous and the development of the thought constant, with regard to a 'de toto' exposition we find ourselves, as we have seen, faced with a certain perplexity, as if the Palatine Master were searching for a personal solution which escaped the difficulty of a realism which is alien to him and threw light on his aversion to the 'vocalism' of the master.[34] The author of *Sententie*, for which it is hard to think of anyone other than the Palatine Master[35], is in an analogous position too; on the one hand his defence of the realist positions appears strange, to say the least, when, in order to solve a difficulty in which the realists have been put by the nominalists, he says that one should assume 'locus' 'in voce' and follows with an analysis directed at basing the value of the logical classifications independently of the plane of things; on the other hand he has recourse to an essentially typically Abelardian distinction of 'significationes', a distinction which is evidently not contained in the opposing nominalism, and still assumes a not very clear position with regard to the 'divisio totius'. There is no logical contradiction among these attitudes: the perplexity arises, however, from the consideration that the description of the opponents made by those who "solum solummodo vocem esse confitentur" does not agree with the author's attitude; he (as is suggested by the 'nos' at the beginning) was to be included among those to whom the nominalistic polemic was addressed. This shows how difficult and delicate it is to conduct an inquiry which throws light on the currents of the 'dialectic' dialogue in the 12th century and which singles out the protagonists and the importance of the positions they held.

REFERENCES

1 *Abaelardiana inedita*, p. xli.

2 This does not seem important to me, however, once Abelard has at times used contradictory terminologies in his inquiries, following the arc of development of his thought. See for example the statements he makes on the problem of universals, Chapter III.

[3] *Op.cit.*, p. 111ff.

[4] *Op.cit.*, p. 112 (7).

[5] See De Rijk's observation: *D.*, p. xxxiii.

[6] *Op.cit.*, p. 112 (1–5).

[7] The procedure in *Ingredientibus* in the confutation of the realist texts is typical.

[8] *Op.cit.*, p. 112 (23). See *D.*, p. 166 (16ff.).

[9] All that we can say about the nominalism of Roscellin derives from evidence about him which is anything but friendly: and especially compared with the Abelardian attitude this appears less critical and worked out.

[10] *Op.cit.*, p. 114 (7).

[11] *Op.cit.*, p. 114 (8ff.).

[12] *Op.cit.*, pp. 114, 115.

[13] *Op.cit.*, p. 114 (7).

[14] See (Chapter III) Abelard's position in *Nostrorum* and the attitude in *Dialectica* with regard to the 'quaestio de toto' (*D.*, p. 549ff.).

[15] *Op.cit.*, p. 115 (22).

[16] *G.L.*, p. 235 (31ff.).

[17] At least, I repeat, from what we know of Roscellin from the Abelardian polemic.

[18] *Op.cit.*, pp. 116–9.

[19] *Op.cit.*, pp. 119–20.

[20] *Op.cit.*, p. 115 (5ff.).

[21] *Op.cit.*, p. 115 (10).

[22] *Op.cit.*, pp. 120 (29)–1 (1).

[23] *Op.cit.*, p. 121.

[24] *D.*, pp. 264–8.

[25] *D.*, p. 268 (25ff.).

[26] *D.*, p. 265 (29ff.); *op.cit.*, p. 121 (14ff.).

[27] *D.*, p. 549ff.

[28] *D.*, p. 554 (37)–5 (9).

[29] *D.*, p. 552 (37)–3 (7); see also *G.G.*, pp. 104–5.

[30] *D.*, p. 553 (8)–4 (36).

[31] *D.*, p. 555 (10–9).

[32] The dispute around the 'totum' was to be a traditional 'quaestio' discussed as usual in the various schools of dialectics, as that 'novissima argumentatio', among others, indicates (*D.*, p. 551 (18)) alluding as it does to a new intervention of the realists which evidently followed a retort from the opposition.

[33] *Op.cit.*, p. 120 (15). Paragraph XXXIII is in fact a reply to the last difficulty posed for the realists by the nominalists (p. 115 (12)), a difficulty, furthermore, which is incompletely expressed in these *Sententie* and which we come across again in *D.*, p. 555 (2–9), this time perfectly expounded.

[34] One should not take this aversion to be radical: Roscellin was nonetheless always the man who had opened up a new path in logical studies (see the evidence of Aventinus: "Roscellinus primus vocum sive dictionum scientiam instituit novam philosophandi viam invenit", contained in Prantl's book, *Geschichte der Logik im Abendlande*, Graz 1955, p. 79, n. 317) and the polemic

that stirred Abelard often has more the meaning of a deepening than of a contrary position being taken up.

[35] As I see it the limit of the certainty of the attribution is in the lack of any strong typical aspect, in the 'quaestio de toto' both of Abelard's position and of that of the author of *Sententie*.

BIBLIOGRAPHY

Abaelardiana inedita (ed. by Minio and Paluello), Rome 1958.

Abelardo, Pietro, *Philosophische Schriften* (ed. by B. Geyer), Munster 1919–33.

—, *Scritti filosofici* (ed. by M. Dal Pra), Milan 1954.

—, *Dialectica* (ed. by L. M. De Rijk), Assen 1956.

Arnold, E., *Zur Geschichte der Suppositionstheorie*, Symposium, Fribourg 1952, pp. 52–134.

Bertola, E., 'Le critiche di A. ad Anselmo di Laon e Guglielmo di Champeaux', *Rivista di filosofia neoscolastica*, 1960, 495–522.

Bird, O., 'The Logical Interest of the Topics as Seen in Abailard', *The Modern Schoolman*, 1959–60, 53–7.

Boehner, Ph., *Medieval Logic*, Chicago 1952, p. 1.

Bréhier, E., *La filosofia del Medio Evo*, Turin 1952, pp. 162–86.

Cottiaux, J., 'La conception de la théologie chez Abélard', *Revue d'histoire ecclésiastique*, 1932, 226.

Cousin, V., *Ouvrages inédits d'Abélard*, Paris 1836, 'Introduction'.

Dal Pra, M., *Op.cit.*, 'Introduction'.

De Rijk, L. M., *Op.cit.*, 'Introduction'.

—, *Logica modernorum*, Assen 1967, Vol. II, Part 1, pp. 186–206.

De Wulf, M., *Storia della filosofia medievale*, Firenze 1945, pp. 198–209.

D'Olwer, L. N., 'Sur la date de la dialectique d'Abélard', *Revue du Moyen Age latin*, 1945, 375–90.

Geyer, B., *Untersuchungen*, in *op.cit.*

Gilson, E., *La philosophie au Moyen Age*, Paris 1944, pp. 278–96.

Giuliani, A., *La controversia*, Pavia 1966, pp. 183–216.

Hauréau, B., *Histoire de la philosophie scolastique*, Paris 1872–80, pp. 362–89.

Moody, E. A., *Truth and Consequence in Medieval Logic*, Amsterdam 1953, pp. 2–4.

Ottaviano, C., *Pietro Abelardo*, Rome 1941, pp. 105–67.

Prantl, K., *Storia della logica in Occidente. Età medievale*, Firenze 1937.

Reiners, J., *Der Nominalismus in der Frühscholastik*, Munster 1910.

Sikes, J. K., *Peter Abailard*, Cambridge 1932, pp. 88–110.

Überweg, F. and Geyer, B., *Die Patristik und Scholastik Philosophie*, Berlin 1928, pp. 213–26, 702.

Vanni Rovighi, S., 'La prima scolastica', in *Grande antologia filosofica*, Milan 1955, pp. 756–81.

Vignaux, P., 'Nominalisme', in *Dictionnaire de théologie catholique*, Paris 1933.

INDEX OF NAMES